THE STRUCTURE OF CONSUMPTION DECISIONS

To my parents

The Structure of Consumption Decisions

A Disaggregated Analysis

VANI K. BOROOAH
Professor of Applied Economics
University of Ulster

Avebury
Aldershot · Brookfield USA · Hong Kong · Singapore · Sydney

Published by
Avebury
Gower Publishing Company Limited
Gower House, Croft Road, Aldershot
Hants. GU11 3HR, England

Gower Publishing Company
Old Post Road, Brookfield, Vermont 05036
USA

British Library Cataloguing in Publication Data

Borooah, Vani K.
The structure of consumption decisions: a disaggregated approach.
1. Great Britain. Consumers. Expenditure
I. Title
339.4'7

Printed and Bound in Great Britain by
Athenaeum Press Ltd., Newcastle upon Tyne.

ISBN 0-566-05772-7

Contents

List of Tables

List of Figures

Acknowledgements

This book was conceived in 1984 when I was employed at the Department of Applied Economics of the University of Cambridge. It was written, four years later, at the Department of Applied Economics and Human Resource Management of the University of Ulster. Over these years I have built up substantial debts of gratitude towards those who took an interest in this work. For their perceptive comments on some of the material presented in this book, my thanks go to participants at seminars at the Universities of Aarhus and Bristol, at the Economic and Social Research Institute, Dublin and to delegates attending session C.47 of the 3rd Congress of the European Economic Association, Bologna. Parts of this book have had prior exposure in academic journals and books. I am grateful to John Wiley and Sons for permission to reproduce material from *Mathematical Methods in Economics* to the Scottish Economic Society for permission to reproduce material from the *Scottish Journal of Political Economy*, to the Royal Economic Society for permission to reproduce material from the *Economic Journal*, and to Academic Press for permission to reproduce material from *Contributions to Political Economy*.

On a more personal level I am grateful to Hashem Pesaran both for the interest he took in this work and also for the use of his estimation routines. Terry Barker and William Peterson commented on the contents of Chapter 3 and John Eatwell on the contents of Chapter 7. To all of them go my thanks. My greatest intellectual debt is however to Don Sharpe with whom I co-authored two of the papers that preceded this book. I have learnt a lot from my conversations with him and much of the material in Chapter 4 owes a great deal to his influence. Needless to say none of these persons are responsible for any residual errors, for which I assume sole liability.

The production of this book has also seen the rapid cumulation of debts. Nial Cairns, as Head of my Department, provided an excellent research environment within the Department and also made available to me every facility for research. Bobbie Coe and Shirley Seal prepared the manuscript for the publishers with considerable expertise. Diana Day and Philip Burch prepared the diagrams. To all of them I am immensely grateful. But my special thanks are reserved for Sharon O'Rawe who typed the entire manuscript, through successive drafts, with the greatest of efficiency and who put up with my frequent changes of mind (and occasional bouts of irritation) with a cheerfulness that never wavered.

Vani K Borooah
University of Ulster
November 1988

are reserved for Sharon O'Rawe who typed the entire manuscript through successive drafts with the greatest of efficiency and who put up with my frequent changes of mind (and occasional bouts of irritation) with a cheerfulness that never wavered.

Vani K. Borooah
University of Ulster
November 1989

1. Introduction

Consumers' expenditure, both in total and in composition, has always been one of the most heavily researched areas of economics. The theory of utility maximization – which continues to provide the conceptual basis for the analysis of such expenditure in neo-classical economics – has its antecedents in work done 100 years ago by Edgeworth (1881), Fisher (1892) and Pareto (1896), though this theory has been considerably refined by the later work of (to name but a few) Slutsky (1915), Hicks (1939), Samuelson (1947), Debreu (1954,1959), Hurwicz and Uzawa (1971) and Diewert (1982). On the empirical front, interest in estimating demand functions dates back to Gregory King's demand curve for wheat in the 17th century. Much empirical work continues to be done in the "pragmatic" tradition of King in which interest is focused on the estimation of individual elasticities without paying too much heed to the niceities of theory. However the major advances in applied consumption work have been in the integration of practice with theory and in the development of analytical tools to enable one to test the validity of the theory. These advances owe much to the work of Stone (1954b), Theil (1965), Barten (1966,1969), Christensen, Jorgensen and Lau (1975) and Deaton and Muellbauer (1979), again to name but a few. No less well researched is aggregate consumers' expenditure and in particular its relation to personal disposable income. This relationship first appeared in Keynes (1936) under the term the "consumption function" and has since been extended and refined by (among others) Modigliani and Brumberg (1954), Friedman (1957), Hall (1978) and Flavin (1981).

Against this background this book focuses on two areas of consumers' expenditure which, inspite of the considerable research effort devoted to the subject (noted above), have, nevertheless, remained relatively neglected. The first is the proper definition of "disposable resources" that influence the consumption and saving decision. The second is the role of income distribution in determining both the composition and the aggregate of consumers' expenditure.

Turning to the first point of focus, the theoretical basis for applied work on the consumption function is provided by hypotheses about the behaviour of individuals and households and not about institutions and businesses. Consequently the relevant income flow for the analysis of consumption decisions should exclude income accruing to the non-household sectors of the economy but should include, as far as is practicable, all the income accruing to the household sector. Several commentators have noted that in this respect the treatment of personal disposable income in the United Kingdom National Accounts (UKNA) has not been perfect. The personal sector in the UKNA is defined to include households, unincorporated businesses, non-profit making bodies (NPMB), unincorporated businesses and life assurance companies and superannuation funds (LASF). Consequently, the UKNA concept of personal disposable income includes the property income of LASF and NPMB, the income of unincorporated businesses (including depreciation, stock appreciation and undistributed profits) but excludes pensions and other benefits paid to households by LASF and excludes any incomes accruing to households from NPMB. It is fairly obvious that this is a far from satisfactory state of affairs, particularly when it is on this concept of personal disposable income that most studies of the UK consumption function have been based.

An additional source of confusion arises from the purely accounting distinction that the UKNA draws between the current, capital and financial accounts of the personal sector. Under this distinction, items relating to consumers' expenditure (current account) precede, in the accounts, items relating to house purchase (capital account) which, in turn, precede items relating to repayment of principal on mortgages (financial account). Unfortunately however, investigators who uncritically use these accounts, are often led to making implicit and perhaps implausible inferences about the actual timing of household decisions. To take a trivial example, it is not unreasonable to suppose that a household deducts from its income its rent or mortgage committments before arriving at a measure of its "disposable resources" available for consumption. Except for mortgage interest, no such prior committment is recognised in studies of UK consumption decisions.

These matters are addressed in chapters 4 and 5 of this book. Chapter 4 sets out a detailed and consistent accounting framework for analysing household decisions and then proceeds to use this framework for arriving at a set of plausible assumptions regarding the sequencing of such decisions. It then proceeds to employ this sequencing structure to define approriate measures of household "disposable resources" and consumption and to construct a set of annual household sector accounts for the period 1966-86, for the UK, based on these definitions. Chapter 5 then re-examines four major, recent studies of the consumption function in the UK – Deaton (1977), Davidson et al. (1978), Hendry and Ungern-Sternberg (1981) and Pesaran and Evans (1984) – in the light of the concepts developed and the data constructed, in the previous chapter. This re-examination shows very clearly that the revised concepts of household "disposable resources" and consumption considerably change the coefficent estimates (and the inferences based upon these estimates) of the original studies, though these changes are by no means implausible.

Chapter 6 examines the role of income distribution in determining consumers' expenditure. Most studies of the consumption function have in common the fact that they ignore distributional considerations in influencing the aggregate volume of consumers' expenditure. Since in Keynes' own analysis (cf. Keynes (1936), ch. 24) emphasis was placed both on the level and on the distribution of disposable income in determining aggregate consumption, this neglect appears surprising. Chapter 6 therefore tests for the presence of distribution effects in the UK consumption function, by estimating directly, separate marginal propensities to consume by income class. This was done by using the Family Expenditure Survey (FES) to construct, over the period 1963-86, annual data on consumption and income by quintile and then, by using this data, to estimate, for each quintile, consumption functions using the "error correction" technique of Davidson et al. (1978). The effect of such an excercise was to suggest that a policy of taxes and transfers that altered the distribution between "rich" and "poor" households, of a given aggregate of disposable income, could, by changing the aggregate volume of consumers' expenditure, have significant macroeconomic consequences.

This theme, namely that of income distribution changes serving as an instrument of macroeconomic policy, is continued in Chapter 7. The focus in this chapter is on the composition, rather than on the total, of consumers' expenditure. The hypothesis here is that, just as the "rich" and the "poor" have different marginal propensities to consume out of disposable income (chapter 6), they also have different consumption patterns and, consequently, different expenditure elasticities for a common set of goods. Therefore a policy of income redistribution would serve to alter not just the aggregate of consumers' expenditure but also its composition. This in turn would have consequences for the pattern of industrial demand and thereby for the balance of payments and the level of employment in the country concerned. Chapter 7 seeks to establish this hypothesis for the UK by estimating the Rotterdam model on data for 10 broad commodity groups, over the period 1963-86, for each quintile seperately, to obtain quintile specific estimates of commodity expenditure elasticities. These estimates are then integrated into the Cambridge Growth Project's industrially disaggregated model of the UK economy, in order to explore the macroeconomic consequences of changes in income distribution. The results point to the fact that there is no contradiction between greater equality and greater efficiency, where the latter is measured by the growth rate of GDP.

Chapters 2 and 3 provide the foundations for the material contained in chapters 4 - 7. Chapter 2 sets out the analytical basis for the theory of consumer demand. This chapter examines the empirical properties of demand functions against the presence (or absence) of which the validity of the theory must be tested and looks at some of the problems that arise in applying a theory of individual behaviour to data based on market outcomes. Another topic that is addressed in this chapter is the intertemporal extension of demand theory to deriving the aggregate consumption function. Chapter 3 attempts to put some empirical flesh to the theoretical skeleton of chapter 2 by discussing the characteristics of the UK data on consumers' expenditure and then using such data to test the validity of the theory of demand based on the notion of the utility maximising consumer. The vehicle for conducting such a test is provided by the Rotterdam model of consumer demand. A part of this chapter is devoted to developing the analytics of this model with a view to making explicit the application of theory to practice. A novel feature of this chapter is the presentation of UK expenditure and own-price elasticity estimates – based on the estimation of the Rotterdam model over the period 1963-86 – for 67 commodities.

The preceding chapters have attempted to provide a thumb-nail sketch of the book in terms of the contents of the individual chapters. At a more general level, this book represents an attempt to carry out a disaggregated study of consumers' expenditure in the UK. Empirical work in the area of consumers' expenditure pay only limited attention to the problems of employing a specification for the aggregate which has only been shown to be plausible for the individual. This procedure is especially disconcerting when the disparate nature of the households that constitute the household sector of the economy is recognised. In the absence of detailed information on individual households, it seems reasonable to consider an analysis at an intermediate level of disaggregation. This is attempted in chapters 6 and 7 where the unit of analysis is households in different income classes rather than the household sector in its entireity. Yet another aspect of the disaggregated nature of this study is the detailed attention paid in chapter 4 to the structure of a household's economic decisions. Typically, in most empirical work, the household's expenditure decision on consumer goods and services is considered in isolation from other economic decisions that it might make. The treatment in this book is a small departure from this tradition. The final aspect of disaggregation lies in the number of commodities considered in the estimation of a consumer demand system for the UK. System estimates are usually available for only a small number of broadly defined commodities. In this respect the disaggregation by 67 commodities, considered in chapter 3, represents an advance on existing studies of consumers' expenditure in the United Kingdom.

2. The theory of consumer choice

2.1 Basic Concepts

The fundamental premise underlying the theory of consumer behaviour (where the consumer could either be an individual or a household) is that the consumer chooses a vector $\mathbf{x}=(x_1...x_n)$ of quantities of the n commodities available, which, in some well defined sense represents his "most preferred" or "best" choice from the set of vectors "feasible" for him. Moreover preferences are typically defined entirely by the consumer's own consumption without reference to the consumption of others. [1] The theory therefore completely identifies choice with preference. This, as has been noted by others (cf. Sen (1979)) is a major limitation of the theory for it cannot account for any motivation for economic action other than pure egotism. A person whose basis for action is so narrow may be rational, in the sense of being an optimizer, but within the exigencies of operating within a social structure, must be regarded as a "rational fool". Be that as it may, it is within the context of this view of *homo economicus* that the theory of consumer behaviour has been developed. The purpose of this chapter is to exposit this theory and, in order to do so, certain concepts have to be defined.

Whether a particular consumption outcome is, or is not, feasible depends on the constraints to which the consumer is subject. These constraints could be both physical and economic:

(i) The vector $\mathbf{x}$ must belong to a set X called the consumption possibility set which is given *a priori* and which will depend on the individual consumer under consideration. The definition of X takes into account all the physical limitations on the consumer's activity; for example, in defining X, the notion of a subsistence standard, either biological or based on social convention, may be taken into account. One of the goods may be labour, that is the consumer, in conjunction with deciding how much of the various goods to buy, also decides on the quantity of labour to supply where this supply is also a determinant of his income.

(ii) In addition the consumer has a limited income, I, and must act within a market where each commodity i has a well defined price p_i. Hence the value of x should not exceed I, that is

$$\sum_{i=1}^{n} p_i X_i \leq I$$

For the model of this chapter, I and the p_i are exogenous.

The consumer's preferences amongst the vectors in X are defined by a real valued function $U(x_1 ... x_n)$ called the utility function, whose domain is the set X. Given two vectors x^1 and x^2 in X, x^1 is preferred (indifferent) to x^2 if and only if $U(x^1) > (=) U(x^2)$. Given a utility level $\bar{U}$ the set R consisting of all points X which yield the utility level $\bar{U}$, that is $R = \{x / U(x) = \bar{U}\}$ defines an indifference locus or curve. The set of all indifference curves corresponding to the different possible utility levels defines an indifference map.

It is also assumed that

1. The set X is closed, convex, bounded from below and contains the null vector. If it contains a vector x^1, it also contains every vector x^2 such that $x_i^2 \geq x_i^1, i=1 ... n$.

Convexity implies that if X contains x^1 and x^2 it contains the line segment joining them. This assumption may be violated if certain goods can only be consumed in integral quantities. Suppose this is the case for good 2 when n=2. Then the set X consists of a number of vertical half-lines as in Figure 2.1. It is not convex since x^3 which lies on the line segment connecting x^1 and x^2 does not belong to X. This situation is obviously not serious when one considers quantities of the first good which contain an appreciable number of units; in such cases X may be reasonably approximated by a convex set.

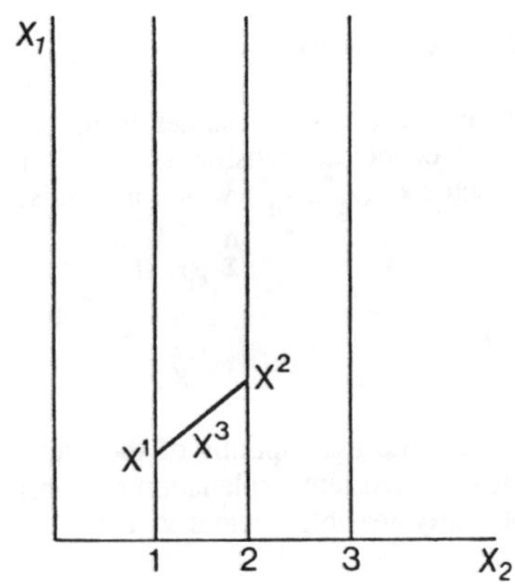

Figure 2.1 Consumption of Integral Quantities

Closure implies that if a sequence of vectors belonging to X converges to a limit, then the limiting vector also belongs to X. In other words the set X is assumed to contain its boundary.

The boundedness condition (which means that there exists a vector $\bar{x}$ such that $x \geq \bar{x}$ for all $x \varepsilon X$) implies that consumption of commodities cannot fall below a prescribed minimum. If the quantity of labour supplied by the consumer is regarded as negative consumption, then the boundedness condition is automatically satisfied if there is an upper limit on the quantity of labour a consumer can supply and if the consumption of other commodities cannot be negative.

The inclusion of the null vector in the feasible set implies – contrary to the notion of a subsistence minimum – that the individual may consume nothing while the last assumption implies that if the consumer has a surplus of commodities over and above what he needs then he can costlessly dispose of the surplus.

2. The utility function $U(x)$, defined on X, is continuous, increasing and twice differentiable. The second property implies that $\partial U(x)/\partial x_i$ – the gain in utility following a small increase in the quantity of commodity i, also called the marginal utility of i – is positive for all $i=1,\ldots n$.

The marginal rate of substitution between good i and j, denoted MRS_{ij}, is the amount by which the quantity of good j must be increased following a small decrease in the quantity of good i in order to leave the utility enjoyed by the consumer unchanged, say at the level $\bar{u}$,

$$MRS_{ij} = \left(-\frac{dx_j}{dx_i}\right)_{u=\bar{u}} = -\frac{\partial U/\partial x_i}{\partial L/\partial x_j}$$

For example, if from given consumption levels of tea and coffee a consumer requires two ounces of coffee to compensate him for the loss of an ounce of tea then the MRS between tea and coffee is 2.

3. The utility function $U(x)$ is "strictly quasi-concave" in the sense that if $U(x^1) \geq U(x^2)$ for two vectors x^1 and x^2, then for every vector x_2 in the line segment (x^1, x^2) (that is $x=ax^1+(1-a)x^2 (0<a<1), U(x)>U(x^1)$. In other words the consumer will prefer an intermediate position to either of two extreme positions although he may be indifferent between these extreme positions.

2.2 The Equilibrium of the Consumer

It is assumed that the objective of the consumer is to choose a consumption vector which, subject to his physical and economic constraints, is "best preferred". An equilibrium for a consumer is therefore a vector $x^*=(x_1^*,\ldots x_n^*)$ which maximises $U(x)$ subject to

$$\sum_{i=1}^{n} p_i x_i \leq I \qquad (2.1)$$

and

$$x \varepsilon X$$

We now show that, under the assumptions of the previous section, an equilibrium exists, so that the theory provides a consistent explanation of consumer behaviour. Consider the set S of physically and economically feasible vectors x. Then S is the intersection of X and the set R satisfying

$$x_i \geq \bar{x}_i \; i=1, \ldots n \qquad (2.2)$$

$$\sum_{i=1}^{n} p_i x_i \leq I \qquad (2.3)$$

where $\bar{x}_i$ $(i=1, \ldots n)$ is the lower bound of asumption 1. Since X is closed and since it can be easily shown that R is closed and bounded, it follows that S is closed and bounded (ie. compact). Also S is not empty since it contains the null vector. Since $U(x)$ is a continuous function defined on a non-empty compact set S, it has a maximum on S, thus establishing the existence of an equilibrium.

Having established the existence of an equilibrium we now turn to its properties. If x^* is an equilibrium consumption vector then

$$\sum_{i=1}^{n} p_i x_i^* = I$$

For if

$$\sum_{i=1}^{n} p_i x_i^* < I,$$

there exists a vector $\mathbf{x}$, all of whose components are greater than the components of $\mathbf{x}^*$, such that

$$\sum_{i=1}^{n} p_i x_i \leq I$$

Then (by assumption 1) $\mathbf{x}$ is in X and also in S; but $U(\mathbf{x}) \geq U(\mathbf{x}^*)$ (by assumption) contradicting the fact that $\mathbf{x}^*$ is an equilibrium.

The first order conditions for a solution to the consumer's problem (with, in view of the above remarks, the inequality in equation (2.3) replaced by an equality) are

$$\frac{\partial U(x)}{\partial x_i} = \lambda p_i, \; i = 1, \dots n, \tag{2.4}$$

$$\sum_{i=1}^{n} p_i x_i = I, \tag{2.5}$$

where λ is the Lagrangian multiplier. Condition (2.4) yields

$$MRS_{ij} = \frac{\partial U(x)/\partial x_i}{\partial U(x)/\partial x_j} = \frac{p_i}{p_j}, \; i, j = 1, \dots n \tag{2.6}$$

so that in equilibrium, the marginal rate of substitution between goods i and j – the rates at which i and j can be substituted maintaining constant utility – should be equal to the ratio of their prices – the rates at which i and j can be substituted maintaining constant income.

The second order conditions are that the quadratic form

$$\sum_{i=1}^{n} \sum_{j=1}^{n} \frac{\partial^2 U(x)}{\partial x_i \partial x_j} dx_i \, dx_j$$

is negative semi-definite for every vector $\mathbf{dx} = (dx1, \dots dxn)$ such that

$$\sum_{i=1}^{n} p_i \, dx_i = 0$$

In other words, in equilibrium, small variations in quantities will not lead to changes in the level of utility but will lead to a fall in the rate of change of utility.

The Lagrangian multiplier, λ, of equation (2.4) can be interpreted as the marginal utility of income since differentiating $U(\mathbf{x})$, applying equation (2.4) and (2.5) and keeping prices constant yields

$$dU = \sum_{i=1}^{n} \frac{\partial U(x)}{\partial x_i} dx_i = \lambda \sum_{i=1}^{n} p_i \, dx_i = \lambda dI$$

It is easily shown that the marginal properties of equilibrium are not altered if the utility function $U(\mathbf{x})$ is replaced by a monotonic increasing transformation of itself, $F(U(\mathbf{x}))$, $F' > 0$. In other words a given utility function represents a preference ordering but not uniquely. The function $F(U(\mathbf{x}))$ represents the same preference ordering, since $F(U(\mathbf{x}^1)) \geq F(U(\mathbf{x}^2))$ if and only if

$U(x^1) \geq U(x^2)$. This is exactly the same as saying that $U(x)$ is an ordinal as opposed to a cardinal utility function.

The first order conditions (2.4) and (2.5) can be solved to yield the (Marshallian) commodity demand functions which express the equilibrium quantities bought, x^* $(i = 1, \ldots n)$ as functions of prices and income:

$$x_i^* = g_i(p_1, \ldots p_n, I) \quad i=1, \ldots n$$

$$= g_i(p, I) \text{ where } p = (p_1, \ldots p_n). \tag{2.7}$$

2.3 Indirect Utility and the Expenditure Function

Consider the consumer's original problem:

$$\text{Maximise } U(x) \text{ subject to } \sum_{i=1}^{n} p_i x_i = I \tag{2.8}$$

and its dual

$$\text{Minimise } I = \sum_{i=1}^{n} p_i x_i \text{ subject to } U(x) = u. \tag{2.9}$$

We can use the same u in both problems, since in the dual we simply use the u which is the maximum attainable in the original problem. Further the outlay in the original is the minimum cost in the dual, since cost minimisation and utility maximisation must imply the same choice. This is a simple consequence of the saddle point theorem. In both problems the optimal values of x are being sought. In the original problem the solution is the set of Marshallian demand functions g_i, (p,I). In the dual problem, the optimal quantities, x_i^* are expressed as a function of prices and utility levels to yield the Hicksian or compensated demand functions, $x_i^* = f_i(p, u)$ and since the solutions coincide

$$x_i^* = g_i(p, I) = f_i(p, u) \tag{2.10}$$

Each of the solutions in (2.10) can be substituted back into their respective problems to yield:

$$U^* = U(x_1^*, \ldots x_n^*) = V(p, I) \tag{2.11}$$

$$I^* = \sum_{i=1}^{n} p_i x_i^* = C(p, u) \tag{2.12}$$

The function $V(p, I)$ defined by (2.11) represents the maximum utility attainable with given prices and income; it is called the indirect utility function. The function $C(p, u)$, defined by (2.12) is the minimum cost of attaining a given utility level with given prices; it is called the expenditure or cost function.

The expenditure and the indirect utility functions are intimately related since inverting $I = C(p, u)$ yields $u = V(p, I)$ and inverting $u = V(p, I)$ yields $I = C(p, u)$.

The expenditure function has five main properties:

(i) The expenditure function is homogenous of degree one in prices, ie. $C(\beta p, u) = \beta C(p, u)$ for any scalar β. This means that given an utility level a proportionate increase in prices rquires an equi-proportionate increase in expenditure to attain that utility level.

(ii) The expenditure function is increasing in u and non-decreasing in **p**. Thus, given prices, to attain a higher utility level requires higher expenditure. Conversely, a given utility level, with higher prices, cannot be attained with lower expenditure.

(iii) The expenditure function is concave in prices so that $C(\beta p + (1-\beta) pq, y) \geq \beta C(p, y) + (1-\beta) C(q, y)$ for two price vectors **p** and **q** and $0 \leq \beta \leq 1$. The intuition behind the concavity of the expenditure function is as follows: let x^* be an expenditure minimizing bundle at prices p^*. Suppose the price of commodity 1 changes from p_1^* to p_1. If the same quantities are bought as before (ie. x^*), costs will be $C = p_1 x_1^* + p_2^* x_2^* + ... p_n^* x_n^*$. However for expenditure minimisation, given a change in price, there will be a change in quantities bought. Hence the expenditure function will lie below the "no change" line and therefore be concave.

(iv) The expenditure function is continuous in **p**.

(v) The Hicksian demand functions may be obtained by differentiating the expenditure function, that is

$$f_i(p,u) = \frac{\partial C(p,u)}{\partial p_i}, \; i = 1, \dots n \quad (2.13)$$

This property is known as the derivative property of the expenditure function.

2.4 The Slutsky Equation

From the first order conditions for consumer's equilibrium, represented by equations (2.4) and (2.5) it can be shown that the following equation, called the Slutsky equation, holds:

$$(\partial g_j(p, I)/\partial p_i) = (\partial g_j(p, I)/\partial p_i)_{u=\bar{u}} - (\partial g_j(p, I)/\partial I)\, x_i^* \quad (2.14)$$

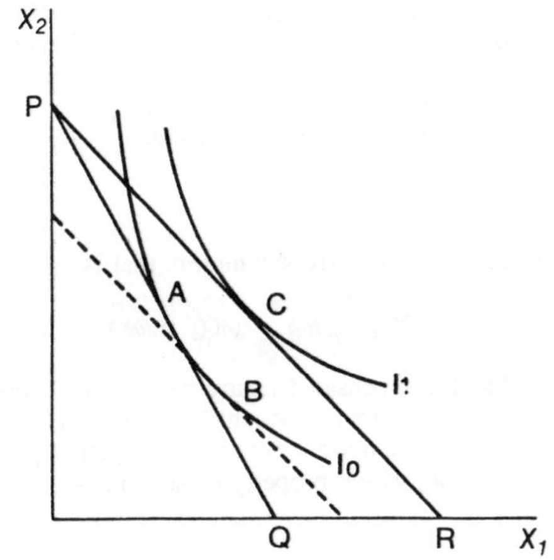

Figure 2.2 Income and Substitution Effects

The Slutsky equation decomposes the demand change induced by the price change (also called the uncompensated price effect) $\partial g_j/\partial p_i$, into two effects:

(i) The substitution effect (or compensated price effect), $\partial f_j/\partial p_i$, whereby the consumer is "compensated" for the change in real income induced by the change in price so that he enjoys the same level of utility as before and responds only to the change in relative prices.

(ii) The income effect, $(\partial g_j/\partial I)x_i$, whereby consumer responds to the change in real income induced by the price change but changes in relative prices (to which he has already responded under (i)) are not considered.

This is illustrated in Figure 2.2, in which A is the original point of equilibrium at which the budget line PQ is tangential to the indifference curve I_o. A fall in the price of good 1 leads to a new budget line PR. If the consumer's income is reduced so that, at the new prices, he obtains the same utility he obtained before the price changes, he is at equilibrium at point B. The movement from A to B is the "substitution effect". The movement from B to C, when at unchanged prices, he responds to higher income, is the "income effect".

2.5 Properties of the Demand Functions

If the demand equations (2.7) were derived from a process of constrained utility maximisation, they would satisfy the following properties.

(i) Adding Up

The total value of the demand is total expenditure, that is,

$$\sum_{i=1}^{n} p_i \, g_i \,(p, I) = I \tag{2.15}$$

In other words, the demand functions have the property that the sum of individual expenditures is exactly equal to total expenditure.

(ii) Homogeneity

The demand functions are homogenous of degree zero in income and prices (since an equi-proportionate increase in prices and income leaves the constraints (2.15) unchanged). This implies that the quantities demanded depend only upon relative prices and real incomes, since a doubling of all prices and income would leave relative prices and real income unchanged and consequently leave the quantities demanded unchanged.

(iii) Symmetry

The compensated cross price derivatives are symmetric, that is,

$$(\partial f_j(p, u)/\partial p_i) = (\partial f_i(p, u)/\partial p_j) \tag{2.16}$$

This means for example, that a compensated penny per pound increase in the price of apples should increase the number of bars of soap bought by a number equal to the number of more pounds of apples bought consequent upon a compensated penny per bar increase in the price of soap. This follows from the derivative property of section 2.3.

(iv) Negativity

The matrix of compensated cross price derivatives is negative semi-definite, that is

$$z'Hz \leq 0, \text{ for any vector } z \tag{2.17}$$

where $H = [\partial f_j/\partial p_i]$ $i,j = 1, \dots n$.

This follows since, by the derivative property, $(\partial f_j \partial p_i) = (\partial^2 C/\partial p_i \partial p_j)$ and the latter is negative semi-definite since $C(p,u)$ is a concave function. In particular the negativity property (iv) implies

$$(\partial f_i/\partial p_i) \leq 0 \;\; i = 1, \dots n, \tag{2.18}$$

that is an increase in the price of a commodity with utility held constant leads to its demand falling (or remaining unchanged).

Now define good i as an inferior good index 1 inferior good if its consumption falls as income rises, that is

$$(\partial g_i/\partial I) < 0 \tag{2.19}$$

For example, one might, as income rises, buy less potatoes and more, say, meat; potatoes in this example would be an inferior good. Then if a good is not an inferior good, by (2.14) its demand must fall as its price rises, that is its uncompensated own price derivative must be negative.

Even if a good is an inferior good the law of demand will hold if the substitution effect outweighs the income effect.

The law of demand will not hold, in which case the relevant good is called a Giffen good, only if the good is an inferior good with the income effect outweighing the substitution effect. An example would again be potatoes. If the price of potatoes falls the consumer can buy as many potatoes as before and still have some money left over with which he can buy meat. However, now that he is buying more meat he does not want as many potatoes as before.

2.6 Market Demand

A significant portion of this book will be concerned with estimating demand relations – of the sort represented by equations (2.7) – and testing to see whether such estimated relationships satisfy the four properties discussed in the previous section. In particular such matters will be the concern of Chapters 3 and 7. However in relating the estimation and testing to the theory of consumer behaviour outlined above, there is one special difficulty. This is the fact that while the theory pertains to the behaviour of a single consumer, be it an individual or a household, the data relates to expenditure on a variety of commodities by an aggregate of consumers. To put the matter differently, the theory is in terms of individual demand but the data is in terms of market demand. A natural line of enquiry is therefore to ask under what conditions would it be possible to treat aggregate consumer behaviour as though it were the outcome of the decisions of a single utility maximising agent. Such a problem, concerning the reconciliation between the "microeconomic" entity of theory and the "macroeconomic" entity of the data, is referred to in the literature as the "aggregation problem". Since this problem will run as an under-current through a great deal of the empirical work reported in the subsequent chapters of this book, it is perhaps timely to discuss some of the "solutions" proposed in the literature to it.

Let x_i^k be the quantity of commodity i bought by the kth consumer, so that the demand functions are:

$$x_i^k = g_i^k(p, I^k) \quad i = 1 \dots n, k = 1 \dots H \tag{2.20}$$

Equations (2.20) implies that total demand x_i, can be written as

$$x_i = \sum_{k=1}^{H} g_i^k(p, I^k) = x_i(I^1 \dots I^H, p) \tag{2.21}$$

In other words, total demand depends not only upon the vector of prices, which is assumed to be the same for all households, [2] but also on the distribution of income between households. To ensure that total demand depends only on aggregate income, and is independent of its distribution, it is necessary to assume that the marginal propensities to spend on each commodity are identical across all consumers, so that

$$(\partial g_i^r/\partial I^r) = (\partial g_i^s/\partial I^s)\ r, s = 1 \ldots H, i = 1 \ldots n \qquad (2.22)$$

Equation (2.22) implies that the demand equations (2.20) must be linear in I^k, so that

$$x_i^k = a_i^k(p) + \beta_i(p)\, I_k \qquad (2.23)$$

where the coefficient on income is not indexed by k.

Equation (2.23) is a condition for exact aggregation, since then

$$x_i = \sum_{k=1}^{H} x_i^k = a_i(p) + \beta_i(p)\, I \qquad (2.24)$$

so that it is possible to treat aggregate consumer behaviour as if it were the outcome of the decisions of a single utility maximising consumer.

In the face of individual consumers maximising their utilities, the conditions for exact aggregation would hold if, and only if, the individual expenditure functions of the consumers were of the Gorman polar form:

$$C^h(U^h, p) = a^h(p) + U^h b(p) \qquad (2.25)$$

which is the cost function for "quasi-homothetic" preferences. The quantity $a^h(p)$ represents the cost of living when utility is zero and hence may be interpreted as the subsistence expenditure of consumer h. Under "quasi-homotheticity" the Engel curves are linear and expenditure elasticities tend to unity as expenditure increases. These are therefore properties that are unlikely to hold for narrowly defined commodities. Consequently if linear aggregation is to work at all, it must only be for broadly defined commodity composites. However, as we shall show in Chapter 6, even at the level of aggregate consumption expenditure there is a systematic variation in the allocation of additional expenditure between "rich" and "poor" consumers. Linearity of demand relations would not therefore appear to be an acceptable supposition. [3]

2.7 Intertemporal Utility Maximisation and the Consumption Function

The previous section looked at the problem of aggregation across consumers in terms of their demands for individual commodities. In this section we analyse the determination of aggregate consumers' expenditure, obtained by aggregating the expenditure of all consumers across all commodities. The theoretical framework for such an analysis is provided by the theory of intertemporal utility maximisation, within the context of the Life Cycle Hypothesis (LCH) of Modigliani and Brumberg (1954), and Ando and Modigliani (1963). Since this hypothesis will provide the backdrop to much of the subsequent discussion in this book on the UK consumption function, it would perhaps be worth setting out its theoretical foundations.

Consider the case of a consumer faced with the problem of maximising utility over two periods, subscripted 1 (present) and 2 (future). His utility function is

$$U = U(C_1, C_2) \qquad (2.26)$$

where C_1 and C_2 are aggregate consumption in periods 1 and 2 respectively.

His budget constraint is given by the condition that the present value of his expenditure on consumption should equal total lifetime wealth the last being defined as the present value of his lifetime income stream plus any assets. Consequently the budget constraint may be written as

$$p_1 C_1 + (p_2/(1+r_2))\, C_2 = W \qquad (2.27)$$

where p_1 and p_2 are consumption prices and r_1 and r_2 are the rates of interest in respectively periods 1 and 2. [4] If A_o represents the level of initial assets and y_1 and y_2 are respectively income in periods 1 and 2 then lifetime wealth, W, is given by [5]

$$W = A_o (1+r_1) + y_1 + (y_2/(1 + r_2)) \tag{2.28}$$

Note that in equations (2.27) and (2.28), the quantities p_2, y_2 and r_2 are, from the point of view of the present, only expected. The simplest solution, adopted here, is to assume that the consumer has single valued expectations for these quantities. Needless to say, when the future is revealed, these expectations may prove to be incorrect.

Maximising the function (2.26) subject to the constraint (2.27) yields a pair of consumption equations

$$C_t = C_t (W, p_1, p_2^*) \qquad t = 1, 2 \tag{2.29}$$

where

$$p_2^* = p_2/(1 + r_2) = p_1[1+(p_2-p_1)/p_1]/(1+r_2) = p_1/(1+r_2^*) \tag{2.30}$$

and

$$1 + r_2^* = 1 + r_2 - ((p_2-p_1)/p_1) \text{ for small enough proportionate changes in prices.} \tag{2.31}$$

C_1, the demand in the current period is in principle immediately effective, while C_2, is demand planned in period 1 for period 2, plans that may not be realised (in period 2) if expectations (held in period 1) relating to p_2, y_2 and r_2 are not fulfilled. The expected real rate of interest is approximated by r_2^*. Figure 2.3 below illustrates the equilibrium of the consumer in this two-period model of intertemporal utility maximisation.

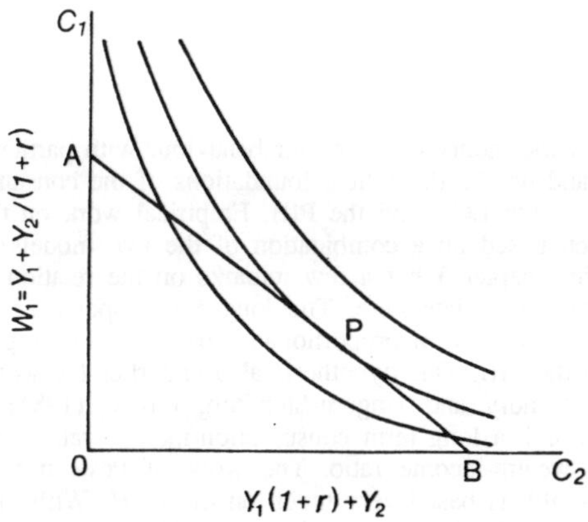

Figure 2.3 Utility Maximisation Over Two Periods

The exogenous determinants of current and future planned consumption are thus present and future incomes, [6] present and future prices, assets and interest rates. An analysis of the comparative statics of changes in these variables, employing the usual distinction between income and substitution effects, can then be carried out. This will not be considered here; [7] instead we turn to a derivation of "conventional" consumption functions from the theoretical framework outlined above.

If it is assumed that the utility function (2.26) is homothetic, so that, for some normalisation of the utility function, doubling quantities doubles utility, [7] then the current period consumption equation takes the LCH form: [9]

$$C_1 = k\,(p_1, p_2^*)\,(W/p_1) \tag{2.32}$$

for some function k(.). Since C_1 is homogenous of degree zero in p_1, p_2^* and W, k(.) is homogenous of degree zero in p_1 and p_2^* and hence depends only on relative prices, $p_1/p_2^*=(1+r_2^*)$. [10] Hence variations in the coefficient of proportionality k, will depend only on variations in the real interest rate; in the absence of such variations, variations in C_1 will be determined solely by variations in real lifetime wealth, W/p_1.

An alternative to the formulation adopted in equation (2.32) is to define y^p as the real income flow generated per period, over an infinite planning horizon, from the stock of wealth, W. [11] Under this definition equation (2.30) becomes

$$C_1 = k(p_1, p_2^*)\,(W/p_1) = K\,(r^*)\,y^p \tag{2.33}$$

Equation (2.33) represents Friedman's (1957) "permanent income hypothesis" (PIH). Under the definition of permanent income, y^p, adopted above, the LCH and the PIH are equivalent for a consumer who, under the LCH, plans his consumption over an infinite life span. [12] However under alternative definitions of permanent income, such as for example that adopted by Friedman (1957),

$$y_t^p = f(y_t, y_{t-1}, y_{t-2} \dots) \tag{2.34}$$

the two hypotheses are not necessarily compatible. [13] The essence of the LCH approach is its "forward looking" aspect while the PIH as represented by equation (2.34) reflects a "backward looking" approach. Indeed the most useful way of viewing the two hypotheses is to view them as essentially rival approaches to the explanation of aggregate consumption behaviour where the two happen to coincide only under a very special definition of permanent income.

2.8 Conclusions

This chapter has discussed the theory of consumer behaviour with particular emphasis on the problems of aggregation and on the theoretical foundations of the consumption function. The latter has been provided by the LCH and the PIH. Empirical work on the UK consumption function has typically been based on a combination of the two models. Details of some of this work are contained in Chapter 5 but a few remarks on the relation between theory and practice might perhaps be appropriate here. The long run property of the Davidson et al. (1978) equation is based on the idea of proportionality between consumption and income and is obviously derived from the PIH. This hypothesis also underlies the work of Deaton (1977). On the other hand, the Hendry and Ungern-Sternberg (HUS) (1981) model incorporates elements of the PIH – through a long term consumption-income ratio – and elements of the LCH – through a target wealth-income ratio. The work of Pesaran and Evans (1984) by emphasising the role of wealth is based very much on the LCH. With these observations we turn in the remainder of this book to an examination of aspects of applied consumption analysis.

NOTES

[1] That is x_i in the vector **x** is the quantity consumed by the consumer of commodity i. The theory could be extended to include the consumption of others but then it would lose its cutting edge since a variety of possibly contradictory behaviour could now be reconciled under "best preference choice" behaviour.

[2] An assumption that may not always be justified (see Piachaud (1974)).

[3] See also Deaton and Muelbauer (1980), Chapter 6.

[4] Note that this relies crucially on the assumption that households are free to lend and borrow without limit, at the same rate of interest, r.

[5] It is assumed here that there are no bequests, that it is $A_2 = 0$. Note also that y_1 and y_2 refer only to labour income since non-labour income is already included in the term $A_0(1+r_1)$.

[6] In a more sophisitcated model labour supply will be determined jointly with consumption so that income will be endogenously determined. See Deaton and Muellbauer (1980), Chapter 12 for an exposition of such a model.

[7] See Deaton and Muellbauer (1980) Chapter 6 for such an analysis.

[8] $U(\lambda C_1, \lambda C_2) = \lambda U(C_1, C_2)$ for some scalar λ

[9] See Modigliani and Brumberg (1954).

[10] From equations (2.30) and (2.31).

[11] That is, $y^p = r^*(W/p_1)$

[12] That is, as the indefinite real income flow associated with real lifetime wealth.

[13] Y^p is the "permanent income" stream expected by the consumer t at time t.

3. Consumers' expenditure in the United Kingdom

3.1 Introduction

The previous chapter set out the elements of the theory that typically underlies the discussion of consumer behaviour in economics. The theoretical problem that was addressed there was one essentially of optimal allocation. In a static context it was one of allocating a given total of expenditure over a number of commodities. In an inter-temporal context it was one of allocating income between consumption and saving over a number of time periods, where, in the case of the Life Cycle Hypothesis, these time periods corresponded to different stages in an individual's life. The determinants of the consumption/saving allocation in the current period then constituted the explanatory variables for the consumption function. This chapter attempts to put come empirical flesh on this theoretical skeleton by applying to it data for the United Kingdom. In doing so it will be useful to preserve the (conceptual) distinction remarked upon above, namely that between the commodity-wise allocation of a given total of consumers' expenditure and the determination of the total itself.

3.2 The Modelling of Consumer Demand

In the previous chapter reference was made to the derivation of demand relations from the theory of constrained utility maximisation. It was further shown there that under the aegis of such a theory the commodity demand functions so derived for the individual consumer would satisfy the four properties of adding up, homogeneity, symmetry and negativity. Although these four properties are fundamental to any attempt at testing the theory, they rely for their verification, on the estimation of a complete system of demand equations. In particular the properties of symmetry and negativity embody constraints **across** the different equations. Early demand studies were however confined to the estimation of demand functions for individual commodities. Although in such studies there was an attempt to integrate practice with theory (Stone (1954a)), such attempts necessarily floundered without a systems-wide approach to the problem.

The earliest means of estimating demand equations as a system, (rather than on an equation by equation basis), was provided by the Linear Expenditure System (LES) of Stone (1954b) and the Rotterdam model of Theil (1965) and Barten (1966, 1969). In spite of the considerable progress made in this field since these early writings (see Deaton and Muellbauer (1980), and Blundell (1988) for useful surveys), the basic distinction continues between systems derived by **algebraically** imposing the theoretical restrictions of adding up, homogeneity, symmetry and negativity on a particular functional form and systems in which the restrictions are tested **statistically** with a general functional form estimated with and without the restrictions imposed. The former approach has the advantage that it saves on degrees of freedom and hence can be applied to a large number of commodities without invoking separability assumptions. It has the disadvantage that since the restrictions are embedded in the system, their empirical validity cannot be statistically tested. Conversely, the latter approach allows the statistical testing of the restrictions implied by demand theory but its application to a large number of commodities requires separability assumptions.

The LES, in which the convenience of a linear functional form, is inseparably allied to the theoretical properties (referred to above) is an instance of the first type of approach. This alliance is obtained in the LES by explicitly maximising the utility function [1]

$$U = \sum_{i=1}^{n} \beta_i \log (x_i - \gamma_i) \tag{3.1}$$

subject to the budget constraint

$$\Sigma p_i x_i = y \tag{3.2}$$

where x_i is the quantity bought of the ith commodity ($i=1 \ldots n$), p_i is its price and y is total expenditure, the β_i and γ_i are parameters ($\Sigma\beta_i=1$) and $x_i > \gamma_i$. This in turn yields (linear) demand equations of the form:

$$p_i x_i = p_i \gamma_i + \beta_i (y - \sum_{j=1}^{n} p_j \gamma_j) \qquad i = 1 \ldots n \tag{3.3}$$

A plausible (and attractive) interpretation of equation (3.3) is to regard γ_i as the subsistence quantity of good i required by the consumer, so that the excess of total expenditure, y, over total subsistence expenditure, $\Sigma\, p_j\, \gamma_j$ is allocated in fixed proportions β_i ($i=1 \ldots n$), over the available goods. Since its discovery by Stone (1954b) the LES has proved one of the most popular means of estimating expenditure systems. The source of its popularity has of course been the convenience of its linear form in estimation, the fact that it is fully consistent with demand theory based on utility maximisation and the fact that this basis in theory, in turn yields considerable parsimony in the number of parameters to be estimated. However, its great drawback is that it does not permit the validity of the restrictions on the demand functions, implied by the theory of utility maximisation, to be tested against data.

In estimating disaggregated consumer demand models, this chapter adopts the second approach where, instead of assuming the validity of the theory, the theory is confronted by the data in order to test its validity. The vehicle used for carrying out such a test is the Rotterdam model, which has been one of the most frequently used models for this purpose. The Rotterdam model, (derived below), essentially explains the real change in the budget share of each commodity by the real change in total expenditure and by changes in the prices of the various commodities. This basic relationship may or may not be estimated with, some or all, the restrictions imposed and likelihood ratio tests may be used to test whether the restrictions are validly imposed.

Early single equation approaches to demand estimation (Stone (1954a)) were based on the choice of a log-linear functional form for the demand relation. This yielded the convenience of allowing the estimated coefficients to be interpreted as elasticities. The Rotterdam model differs from the log-linear approach in that it works in differentials of logarithms rather than in levels.

Specifying a demand function in logarithms yields:

$$\log x_i = \alpha_i + e_i \log y + \sum_{j=1}^{n} e_{ij} \log p_j \qquad (i = 1 \ \ldots \ n) \tag{3.4}$$

To obtain the Rotterdam model, differentiate totally equation (3.4) to obtain

$$d\log x_i = e_i \, d\log y + \sum_j e_{ij} \, d\log p_j \qquad (i = 1 \ \ldots \ n) \tag{3.5}$$

where, of course, e_i is the expenditure elasticity of commodity i and e_{ij} is the price elasticity of commodity i with respect to commodity j (i, j=1 ... n).

Slutsky's rule [2] gives us

$$\left.\frac{\partial x_i}{\partial p_j}\right|_{u=\bar{u}} = s_{ij} = \frac{\partial x_i}{\partial y} x_j + \frac{\partial x_i}{\partial p_j} \qquad (i,j = 1 \ \ldots \ n) \tag{3.6}$$

from which it follows

$$e_{ij} = e_{ij}^{*} - e_i w_j \tag{3.7}$$

where $w_j = (p_j x_j)/y$ is the budget share of the jth commodity and the e_{ij}^* are the compensated price elasticities.

Substituting (3.7) into (3.5) yields

$$d\log x_i = e_i(d\log y - \sum_j w_j \, d\log p_j) + \sum_j e_{ij}^* \, d\log p_j \qquad (i = 1 \ \ldots \ n) \tag{3.8}$$

Symmetry restrictions ($s_{ij}=s_{ji}$) cannot be imposed on (3.8) since this implies

$$s_{ij} \frac{p_i p_j}{y} = w_i e_{ij}^{*} = w_j e_{ji}^{*} = s_{ji} \frac{p_i p_j}{y} \tag{3.9}$$

and this involves the variable budget shares.

To allow the imposition of symmetry, equation (3.8) can be multiplied by w_i to yield

$$w_i \, d\log x_i = b_i \sum_{j=1}^{n} w_j \, d\log x_j + \sum_{j=1}^{n} c_{ij} \, d\log p_j \tag{3.10}$$

where

$$b_i = w_i e_i = p_i \frac{\partial x_i}{\partial p_i} \tag{3.11}$$

$$c_{ij} = w_i e_{ij}^{*} = \frac{p_i p_j}{y} s_{ij} \tag{3.12}$$

and $d\log y - \sum w_j \, d\log p_j = \sum w_j \, d\log x_j$.

In terms of the **empirical** work, which is based on discrete time, the above equation is defined in slightly modified form as follows:

$$\bar{w}_{it} \, \Delta\log x_{it} = b_i \sum_{j=1}^{n} \bar{w}_{jt} \Delta\log x_{jt} + \sum_{j=1}^{n} c_{ij} \, \Delta\log P_{jt} + v_{it}$$

$$t = 1 \ldots 26 \ (1963\text{-}86), \ i = 1 \ \ldots \ n \tag{3.13}$$

where

Δ is the first difference operator $\bar{w}_{it} = (w_{it} + w_{it-1})/2$
v_{it} is the disturbance term such that $E(v_{it})=0$,
$E(v_{it} v_{js}) = \omega_{ij}$ if $t = s$
$= 0$ otherwise

Equation (3.13) can be estimated with an intercept term. When an intercept term is included it is to be interpreted as an autonomous change in tastes. The system of equations represented by (3.13) is the Rotterdam model and may be interpreted as follows.

1) The dependent variable, $w_i \text{dlog} x_i$, is the change in the budget share of the ith commodity caused by a change in the quantity bought of the ith commodity. Note that the budget share can change if either x_i, p_i or y changes $(dw_i = w_i \text{dlog} p_i + w_i \text{dlog} x_i - w_i \text{dlog} y)$. The dependent variable isolates the first type of change.
2) The explanatory variable, $\Sigma\, w_j \text{ dlog} x_j$, is to be interpreted as the proportionate change in total real expenditures. Again a change in total nominal expenditures may be due to either a change in real expenditures or a change in prices $(\text{dlog} y = \Sigma w_i \text{dlog} x_i + \Sigma w_i \text{dlog} p_i)$. The explanatory variable, $\Sigma w_j \text{dlog} x_j$, isolates the first type of change.
3) The explanatory variables $\text{dlog} p_j$ $(j=1 \ldots n)$ are of course the proportionate price changes. When the homogeneity restriction is imposed, these become relative price changes.
4) The coefficients b_i are marginal expenditure of commodity i $(b_i = w_i e_i = \partial(p_i x_i/\partial y)$. To obtain the expenditure elasticities, e_i, divide the marginal expenditures, b_i, by the budget share w_i. Since w_i varies over time, so will e_i. In this chapter the elasticities are quoted for the final year of the estimation period, 1981. Similarly, the coefficients c_{ij} when divided by the budget shares w_i yield the compensated price elasticities, e_{ij}^*; these too are time-variant and quoted in this chapter for 1986.
5) In summary therefore the Rotterdam model explains the 'real' change in the budget shares of the commodities by the change in total real expenditure and by the changes in (relative) prices.

The restrictions implied by demand theory (adding up, homogeneity, symmetry and non-negativity) can be imposed on the system represented by equation (3.10).

Adding up requires that

$$\sum_i p_i x_i = y \tag{3.14}$$

Differentiating both sides of (3.14) with respect to y yields

$$\sum_i p_i \frac{\partial x_i}{\partial y} = \Sigma w_i e_i = 1 \tag{3.15}$$

Then differentiating (3.14) with respect to p_j yields

$$\Sigma p_i \frac{\partial x_i}{\partial p_j} + x_j = 0 \tag{3.16}$$

$$\text{Now } \sum_i p_i s_{ij} = \sum_i p_i \left[\frac{\partial x_i}{\partial y} x_j + \frac{\partial x_i}{\partial p_j} \right] = x_j \sum_i p_i \frac{\partial x_i}{\partial y} + \sum_i p_i \frac{\partial x_i}{\partial p_j} = x_j - x_j = 0$$

(using (3.15) and (3.16)).
In turn $\sum_i p_i s_{ij} = 0$ implies

$$\sum_i w_i e_{ij}^* = 0 \tag{3.17}$$

Hence additivity requires

$$\Sigma b_i = 1 \text{ and } \sum_i c_{ij} = 0 \qquad (j = 1 \ldots n) \tag{3.18}$$

The restrictions embodied in (3.18) have an obvious interpretation. The b_i are the marginal propensities to consume and one of the requirements of additivity is that these propensities should sum to unity. The other requirement is that the net effect of a price change on the budget should be zero. This in turn requires restrictions on the $c_{ij}(i, j=1 \ldots n)$.

Homogeneity requires that an equi-proportionate change in prices and income leaves the quantities demanded unchanged. Since, when all prices and income change by the same factor, the cheapest bundle yielding utility u is unchanged, Hicksian demand functions, [3] $h_i(u, p)$ are homogeneous of degree zero in prices, ie.

$$h_i(u, \lambda p) = h_i(u, p) \tag{3.19}$$

By Euler's theorem

$$\sum_j \frac{\partial h_i}{\partial p_j} p_j = \sum_j s_{ij}\, p_j = 0 \tag{3.20}$$

and since $c_{ij} = \frac{p_1}{y} p_j\, s_{ij}$, homogeneity requires

$$\sum_j c_{ij} = 0 \tag{3.21}$$

The **symmetry** of the substitution matrix $(s_{ij}=s_{ji})$ requires

$$c_{ij} = c_{ji} \tag{3.22}$$

and the **negative semidefiniteness** of the substitution matrix $S=(s_{ij})$ requires in turn, by virtue of the fact that all prices are positive, that the matrix $C=(c_{ij})$ be negative semidefinite.

The Rotterdam model could be regarded as a special case of the more general case of "flexible functional forms". In this general case the basic strategy is to approximate the underlying expenditure or (direct or indirect) utility functions by a functional form that can be regarded as a reasonable approximation. As Theil (1980) shows, the Rotterdam model can be regarded as a finite change approximation to the solution to Barten's (1969) fundamental matrix equation expressed in infinitesimal changes. Other examples of "flexible functional forms" are the "indirect translog" model of Christensen, Jorgensen and Lau (1975) which is an approximation to an unknown indirect utility function and the "almost ideal demand system" (Deaton and Muellbauer (1980)) which uses an approximation to an unknown expenditure function.

3.3 The Commodity Groupings and the Data

Blundell (1988) noted that "the ability to group commodities by type or time period stands as one of the most valuable forms of restrictions on consumer preferences ... if consumers optimise at all, they probably will use some form of grouping to enable some simplification of the decision making process". The method of grouping most widely used in the empirical work on demand analysis rests on Gorman's (1959) hypothesis of two-stage budgeting. Under this hypothesis consumers first allocate their expenditure to broad commodity groups and then to expenditure within these groups. [4] A utility maximising consumer's ability to undertake such multi-stage budgeting depends on his utility function being weakly separable in its arguments. By this is meant that preferences can be represented as:

$$U = U(x_1 \ldots x_n) = U[U_1(x^1) \ldots U_m(x^m)] \tag{3.23}$$

where x^k refers to the vector of quantities of commodities in group k and $U_k(x^k)$ is the subutility function defined over commodities in group k, $k=1 \ldots m$.

An important implication of weakly separable utility functions is that the marginal rates of substitution between any two goods in a particular group is independent of the quantities consumed of commodities not in that group. This property then facilitates the second stage of the decision making process by enabling within group allocations to be determined solely by within group prices and by the expenditure allocated to that group from the earlier stage of decision making.

In applying the Rotterdam model of consumers' expenditures (encapsulated by equation (3.13)) to UK data for 67 commodities over the 26 year period, 1963-86, the hypothesis of two stage decision making proved invaluable. The estimation of the system in the presence of such a large number of commodities could not otherwise have been achieved without running into a severe "degrees of freedom" problem. The solution to this problem lay in grouping the 67 commodities into 11 broad groups, thereby splitting the consumers' budgetary allocation decision into two stages. At the first stage, total expenditure was allocated between the broad groups using appropriately defined group price indices; at the second stage the within group allocations were determined using only the allocated group expenditure and the within group prices. The remainder of this section describes the nature of the consumers' expenditure data and the consumption groupings employed in estimating the Rotterdam model.

The United Kingdom National Accounts (UKNA) introduced, in 1983 after 25 years of little change, a new classification of consumers' expenditure. Broadly the changes meant that consumers' expenditure was now to be classified according to the purpose of expenditure whereas the earlier classification was partly based on purpose and partly on the nature of the goods and services. Another sweeping change was that the expenditure on goods and services by private non-profit making bodies (NPMB) was now separated from household expenditure. Expenditure on the various commodities now related only to households (including unincorporated businesses) and the aggregate expenditure by NPMB was shown separately. Earlier, expenditures by NPMB were included with household expenditures on the various goods and services, though wages and salaries paid by NPMB and their capital consumption were separately identified.

Consumers' expenditure data on this new classification is available from the CSO, in both current and constant (1980) prices, on an annual basis, from 1963 and it was on this data that the estimation of the Rotterdam model – the results of which are reported in the following section – were based. On the basis of this data the commodities were grouped into 11 groups, reflecting it was hoped, major items in the consumers' budget. These groups were: Food; Vices; Clothing and footwear; Housing; Fuel and power; Durable goods; Household goods; Transport; Communications; Recreational goods and services; Other goods and services. The detailed commodity composition of these groups are shown in Table 3.1. The budget shares for these commodity groups are shown in Table 3.2 for selected years of the period 1965-86. This shows that, in 1986, the most important item in the UK's consumption budget was housing (with a budget share of 15.6 per cent) followed by Other goods and services (14.8 per cent), Food (14.5 per cent), Vices (10.8 per cent), and Transport (10.2 per cent). The relative budget shares in these items have changed dramatically in the past 20 years or so. Thus in 1965 it was Food (with a budget share of 22.2 per cent) that was the dominant item in the consumers' budget followed by Vices (12.9 per cent), Other goods and services (12.2 per cent) and Housing (11.2 per cent).

These changes have been caused by an amalgam of several factors – some to do with changes in consumer behaviour and others to do with the definitions adopted for the commodity categories. The falling budget share for food over the past 20 years has much to do with its low expenditure elasticity (cf. Table 3.3). Thus over the period 1965-86, total household real (in constant 1980 prices) consumption expenditure rose by 60 per cent while, over the same period, total household real expenditure on food items rose by only 13 per cent. Changing consumer tastes had much to do with the evolution of the budget share for food: between 1965-86 the consumption of meat and bacon in the UK rose by only 2 per cent and in the last eight years of this period, consumption of such items actually fell by 7 per cent; consumption of fish, oils and fats and sugar fell over the entire period by respectively 12, 9 and 51 per cent while increases of 190, 37 and 20 per cent were recorded by soft drinks, other manufactured food and preserves and confectionery respectively. [5]

Changing consumer tastes also had much to do with the fall of 2 percentage points in the budget share of "vices" over 1965-86. This was almost entirely caused by the fact that the consumption of cigarettes fell by 24 per cent over the period. Although consumption of the alcoholic drinks component of "vices" increased by 81 per cent (beer: 26 per cent, spirits: 114

Table 3.1
The Commodity Groups and Their Components

Group 1: Food

Bread and cereals; Meat and bacon; Fish; Dairy products; Oils and fats; Fruit; Beverages; Potatoes and vegetables; Sugar and preserves; Other manufactured food.

Group 2: Vices

Beer; Spirits; Wine; Cider and sherry; Cigarettes; Other tobacco.

Group 3: Clothing and Footwear

Men and boys' wear; Women, girls' and infants' wear; Footwear.

Group 4: Housing

Imputed rent of owner-occupiers; Other rents; Rates; Sewage and water charges; Do-it-yourself goods; Contractors charges and insurance (however payments made by occupiers to contractors for improvements are no longer included).

Group 5: Fuels

Electricity; Gas; Coal and coke; Other fuels.

Group 6: Durable Goods

Furniture, pictures etc. (now includes nursery furniture and perambulators, pictures and dealers' margins on second-hand furniture); Carpets and other floor coverings; Household appliances ("white" goods); Cars, motor cycles and other vehicles (including cycles and caravans); Television, radio and other durable goods ("brown" goods – includes photographic and optical equipment).

Group 7: Household Goods

Textiles and soft furnishings; Hardware; Cleaning materials (excluding toilet soap).

Group 8: Transport

Petrol and oil; Vehicle excise duty; Other running costs of motor vehicles; Rail travel; Bus and coach travel; Air travel; Other travel (includes removals and storage and travel agent commissions).

Group 9: Communications

Postal service; Telecommunications.

Group 10: Recreational Goods and Services

Television and video hire charges, licence fees and repairs; Sports goods, toys, games and camping equipment; Other recreational goods (records and tapes, horticultural goods, pets and pet food); Betting and gaming (including expenditure on jackpot machines in non-profit-making clubs); Other recreational and entertainment services (cinema and other admissions); Books; Newspapers and magazines; Expenditure abroad by UK residents.

Group 11: Other Goods and Services

Domestic and household service (includes repairs and hire of household appliances, laundry and dry cleaning, window cleaning and chimney sweeping and house contents insurance); Education (includes university fees and private school fees even if such schools are registered charities); Chemists' goods (pharmaceutical products and medical equipment); Health (NHS payments and medical expenses); Toilet articles and perfumery (includes toilet soap); Hairdressing and beauty care; Jewellery, silverware, watches and clocks; Other goods (travel goods, stationery, fancy goods and income-in-kind); Catering (meals and accommodation – includes payments by residents of old peoples' homes to local authorities); Other services (includes accident and miscellaneous insurance).

Table 3.2
Budget Shares in the UK of 11 Broad Commodity Groups: 1965-86

	percentage of total consumers' expenditure				
	1965	1970	1975	1980	1986
Food	22.2	20.2	18.5	16.8	14.5
Vices	12.9	12.8	11.8	10.9	10.8
Clothing & footwear	9.2	8.8	8.1	7.3	7.3
Housing	11.2	12.4	13.5	13.8	15.6
Fuel	4.7	4.7	4.5	4.7	5.1
Durables	8.3	8.2	9.1	10.1	8.0
Household goods	2.8	2.7	2.5	2.3	2.1
Transport	7.6	8.9	9.5	10.2	10.2
Communications	1.0	1.1	1.4	1.7	1.9
Recreational goods & services	7.9	8.3	8.9	9.3	9.7
Other goods & services	12.2	11.9	12.2	12.9	14.8
	100	100	100	100	100

Source: United Kingdom National Accounts

per cent, wine: 290 per cent) over 1965-86 this was not enough to enable overall real expenditure on "vices" to grow by more than 33 per cent over the period. Other goods and services, in direct contrast to "vices", recorded a 2 percentage points increase in its budget share over this period. The contribution here came from an almost five-fold increase in the consumption of "other services". The categories recreational goods and services and transport also showed comparable improvements in their budget shares. In the case of the former this was largely contributed to by a 100 per cent increase in real expenditure abroad by UK households, by a 150 per cent increase in real expenditure on other recreational goods (mostly on records and tapes), by a 237 per cent increase in real expenditure on sports goods and by a 260 per cent increase in real expenditure on television and video hire charges and television licence fees. Counteracting these spectacular increases (and perhaps serving as a comment on the times in which we live) real expenditure on books rose by only 10 per cent over 1965-86 (and actually fell by 17 per cent over 1980-86) while real expenditure on newspapers and magazines fell by 25 per cent over the period.

In the case of transport, most of the increases in its budget share have been due to increased real expenditure on the running of motor vehicles (eg. real expenditure on petrol and oil increased by 134 per cent over 1965-86), and to increased real expenditure on air travel. Over 1965-86 real expenditure on air travel rose (in 1980 prices) from £311 million in 1965 to £2226 million in 1986. Counteracting this increased popularity of air transport and of private surface transport was the declining popularity of public transport. Real expenditure on rail travel increased by only 18 per cent over 1965-86 while that on bus and coach travel fell by 50 per cent.

The above discussion has focused on changes in real consumption patterns contributing to changes in budget shares. Such shares may of course also change owing to different rates of price increases for the different commodities. The category clothing and footwear provides an instance of price factors dominating budget share changes. The budget share of clothing and footwear fell from 9.2 per cent in 1965 to 7.3 per cent in 1986 even though in real terms consumption on every item in this category [6] increased by more than the overall increase of 60 per cent in household real consumption expenditure. This is because over the same period the price index for total household expenditure rose by 531 per cent while the price index for clothing and footwear rose by only 284 per cent.

Housing provides another instance where price effects have dominated movements in budget shares. Table 3.2 shows that the budget share for housing in 1986 was 4 percentage points up on its 1965 value, inspite of the fact that over the period, real expenditure on housing increased by only 53 per cent. The explanation for this sharp rise in the budget share of housing expenditure lies in the fact that between 1965 and 1986, the price index for such expenditure rose by over 800 per cent in contrast to, as noted above, a general increase in prices of 531 per cent. In determining housing expenditure the UKNA imputes a rent payment to owner-occupiers which they presumably would have paid had they rented their dwelling from a landlord. [7] With the spread of owner occupation the real value of such imputed rents doubled between 1965 and 1986, while the rise in property values meant that the price index associated with such rents rose by 831 per cent. Real expenditure on non-imputed rents actually declined slightly between the same years, though the price index associated with such rents increased by over 900 per cent. Housing therefore is a commodity group on which overall there have been relatively small increases in real expenditure over the past two decades. The rise in the budget share for this group has been almost entirely caused by price factors.

A discussion of trends in commodity group budget shares would not be complete without a reference to consumer durable goods, for though the budget share for this broad category is not dissimilar in 1986 to that prevailing in 1965, Table 3.2 shows that the intervening years have displayed a steady rise in its share till 1980, with a gradual fall thereafter.Moreover behind the gradual movements in the aggregate budget share, lies considerable turbulence in the consumption of the individual commodities in this group. Thus for example after a 33 per cent increase between 1965 and 1973, real expenditure on furniture virtually stagnated over the 1974-86 period. Real expenditure on carpets showed hardly any change between any years of the 1965-86 period. By way of contrast real expenditure on major household appliances ("white" goods) increased by 91 per cent between 1965 and 1973 and by over 100 per cent between 1974 and 1986. Demand for motor vehicles did not fare so well, with real expenditure on this category increasing by 146 per cent over the entire 1965-86 period. The real success in the durables goods category over the past twenty years has undoubtedly been television, videos and other "brown" goods. In 1965 real expenditure on such items was £418 million; by 1986 it had increased ten-fold to £4159 million. Although expenditure on television and audio equipment had increased steadily since 1965, the advent of video recorders in the earlier 1980s proved to be a watershed. In the five years between 1982 and 1986 real expenditure on "brown" goods increased from its 1982 value of £2115 million by just under £2000 million. A combination of such trends in the real consumption of the various durable goods with movements in their respective prices then served to provide movements in the budget share, summarised in Table 3.2, for the broad category.

This section discussed a number of topics, first of which was the importance of the assumption of multi-stage decision making in applied consumption analysis and the theoretical basis for such an assumption. It then went on to discuss the characteristics of the data, firstly in terms of the grouping of the individual commodities into broad categories (so as to facilitate the process of hierarchical decision making) and then in terms of movements in the budget shares of these categories, and their constituent commodities, over the period 1965-86. In examining inter-temporal movements in commodity budget shares, it was pointed out that these could be caused by variations in the quantities consumed of the various commodities and/or by variations in their prices. In the context of the UK experience the former effect was dominant for some commodities and the latter effect was dominant for others. With these observations the next section turns to an analysis of consumption behaviour (disaggregated by commodity) in the UK using the Rotterdam model, the mechanics of which were developed in the previous section.

3.4 Estimating and Testing the Rotterdam Model

The Rotterdam Model of consumer demand, as noted in section 3.2, seeks to explain, within the context of a system of demand equations, the "real" change in a commodity's budget share in terms of changes in commodity relative prices and changes in total "real" consumption expenditure. As a consequence it abstracts from budget share changes caused by relative differences in the commodity inflation rates. These are taken as exogenously given. The emphasis on estimating an equation system (as opposed to estimating individual equations independently of one another) enables the cross-equation restrictions of demand theory (viz. symmetry and negativity) to be imposed and their validity to be statistically tested.

The Rotterdam model was, in this chapter, first estimated on data for the broad commodity groups, listed in the previous section, and then on data for each group separately. The period of estimation was 1963-86 and the source of the data was the consumer expenditure accounts in the UKNA. In each case, the restrictions of demand theory were imposed in the sequence: no restrictions (NR), homogeneity (HM), homogeneity and symmetry (HMSY) and homogeneity, symmetry and negativity (HMSYNG) and the system of demand equations, for the relevant group, estimated subject to the appropriate constraints. The results of testing the validity of these restrictions, using likelihood ratio tests, are reported in Appendix 3.2. For the broad groups none of the restrictions could be accepted (Appendix 3.2, Table 3.4) and this was consistent with the findings of Barten (1969), Byron (1970) and Baldwin, Hadid and Philips (1983). The results reported in this chapter therefore constitute further evidence of the general lack of support provided by data to the inferences of demand theory.

The results for the within group testing (Appendix 3.2, Tables 3.5-3.15) do not, however, tell such a consistent story. For 6 of the 11 groups, (namely vices, clothing and footwear, housing, household goods, transport and communications) the combined restrictions of homogeneity and symmetry could not be rejected, though occasionally this non-rejection was only achieved a the 1 per cent level of significance. For 4 out of the remaining 5 groups (namely fuels, durable goods, recreational goods and services and other goods and services) all the restrictions were unequivocally rejected. For the food group, the basic restriction of homogeneity was not rejected though symmetry could not be accepted, either with or without homogeneity.

For reasons to do with economy of space, the estimation results are shown only in summary form with the emphasis being on the two major parameters of interest, namely the expenditure and the own-price elasticities. These are shown for the broad groups in Table 3.3 and for the narrow groups in Appendix 3.3, Tables 3.16-3.26. In each case these elasticities relate to the situation in which all the demand restrictions were in force. In other words equations (3.11) and (3.12) define the relationship between the coefficients and the expenditure and compensated price elasticities; equation (3.7) defines the uncompensated price elasticities. All elasticity estimates relate to 1986 and are the values implied by utility maximising behaviour.

Table 3.3
Expenditure and Own Price Elasticities for the Broad Groups

	Expenditure elasticity	Compensated price elasticity	Uncompensated price elasticity	Budget share for 1986(%)
Food	0.584*	-0.015	-0.100	14.48
Vices	0.943*	-0.613*	-0.715	10.84
Clothing & footwear	1.360*	-0.620*	-0.718	7.25
Housing	0.268*	-0.030	-0.072	15.55
Fuel	0.526	-0.328*	-0.355	5.06
Durable goods	3.788*	-0.039	-0.343	8.03
Household goods	0.993*	-0.651	-0.672	2.13
Transport	0.757*	-0.212*	-0.289	10.22
Communications	0.760*	-0.163*	-0.177	1.94
Recreational goods & services	0.994*	-0.985*	-1.081	9.66
Other goods & services	0.895*	-0.063	-0.195	14.84

* = coefficient estimates that were twice their standard error

The estimates of the slope coefficients conformed broadly to a priori expectations. Among the broad groups all the estimated expenditure elasticities were positive and, except in the case of fuels, were all significantly different from zero (Table 3.3). Only two of the estimated expenditure elasticities were greater than unity – for clothing and footwear and for durable goods. The expenditure elasticity for durable goods was remarkably high and was undoubtedly influenced by the post-1981 "video boom", discussed in the previous section. In fact expenditure elasticity estimates based on data upto 1981, yielded a value for durable goods of only 1.7 (cf. Borooah (1985)). The imposition of negativity ensured that all the own-price effects were correctly signed. Among the broad groups six of the estimated own-price elasticities were significantly different from zero. The fact that in this group were included vices, clothing and footwear, fuel, transport, communications and recreational goods and services, seemed eminently plausible.

Turning to the commodity estimates (Appendix 3.3, Tables 3.16-3.26), it is obvious that changes in real expenditure continued to play a significant role in determining "real" changes in budgetary shares. Of the estimated expenditure elasticities for the sixty two commodities, all were positive and forty four were significantly different from zero; the corresponding figure for the own-price elasticities was forty five. The highest expenditure elasticities were obtained for DIY goods (5.2), TV, radio etc. (4.5), coal and coke (3.4) contractors' charges on housing (3.3), other manufactured food (2.8) and motor cars (2.0). The commodity own-price elasticities were all correctly signed (ie. negative) and the highest values were recorded for Carpets (-2.9), Betting and Gaming (-1.9) and Furniture (1.6).

Finally the equations were all estimated with an intercept term included among the explanatory variables. As was noted earlier in section 3.2, this term is to be interpreted as an autonomous change in tastes exercising an influence on budget shares over and above that exercised by real expenditure and relative price changes. Among the broad groups, the estimated coefficient on this term was significantly different from zero (and positive) for housing and transport. [8] In the food group, oils and fats had a negative estimate on the intercept term that was significantly differently from zero, while potatoes and vegetables had a corresponding positive estimate. Amongst "vices", both wines and cigarettes had respectively positive and negative "significant" intercept estimates. In the housing group, "expenditure" on imputed rent and on DIY goods had positive and significant intercept estimates. Amongst fuels, electricity and gas had positive, significant intercept estimates, while for coal and coke and other fuels they were negative and significant. The case of coal and coke is interesting in that it has a high expenditure elasticity in tandem with an autonomously declining budget share. This is probably a comment on the income levels of persons using the fuel. Amongst durables, the intercept was positive and significant for television and videos and negative and significant for motor cars. In the transport group, bus and coach travel had a significant negative intercept estimate. There were no other commodities in the other groups with significant autonomously declining or increasing "real" budget shares.

3.5 Aggregate Consumers' Expenditure

The preceding sections discussed trends in consumers' behaviour in the UK with respect to expenditure on individual commodities and to expenditure on groups of such commodities. This section turns to a discussion of trends in aggregate consumers' expenditure with a view to providing a rough sketch of the empirical background against which the discussion of the following three chapters – which take as their province the modelling of the aggregate consumption function – will be conducted.

One strand of economic interest in the UK has been the influence of movements in the inflation rate on movements in the saving ratio. In particular the coincidence, in the UK, of high inflation rates with high saving ratios in the 1970s was remarked upon and several models were proposed to link the two phenomenon. As Deaton (1983) remarked, the more sophisticated of such analysis recognised the theoretical indeterminacy of the effect of inflation on saving and appealed to the empirical evidence. [9]

As regards such evidence the first point that could usefully be made is that the inexorable process of data revision has resulted in the official statistics assigning, in 1988, much lower saving ratios to the 1970s than they did in 1978. Figure 3.1 plots the personal saving ratio from three separate editions of the UK Central Statistical Office's publication *Economic Trends Annual Supplement* (ETAS) for the period 1970-80. Superimposed on these ratios is the inflation rate. The downward revisions to the saving ratio that have been made over the past few years is a striking feature of Figure 3.1. Thus the saving ratio reported for 1975 in the 1979 edition of ETAS was 15.0 per cent. This was reduced to 12.4 per cent in the 1982 edition and then to 12.3 in the 1988 edition. For the 1970-77 period, the 1979 edition of ETAS reported an average saving ratio of 12.26 per cent, with a standard deviation of 2.64. The corresponding figures for the 1988 edition were 10.48 per cent and 1.49 and the correlation between the saving ratios from these two different editions of ETAS for the period was 0.902.

Movements in the personal saving ratio, inflation and the rate of growth in real personal disposable income are charted in Figure 3.2 for the period 1970-86. Three features of the

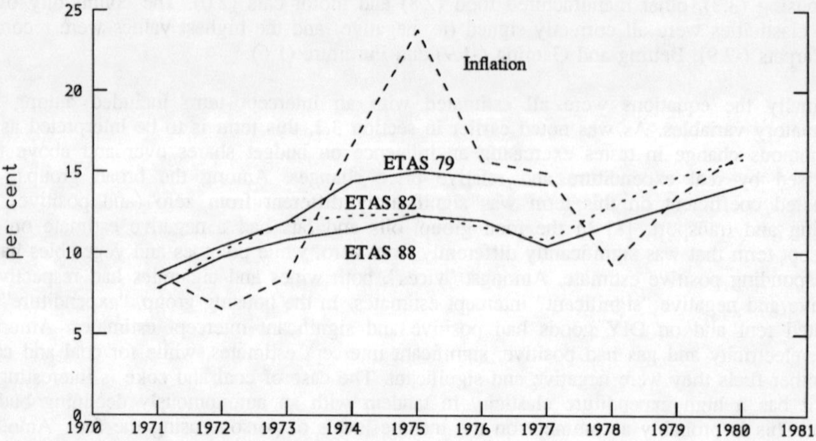

Figure 3.1 Revisions to the Saving Ratio, 1971-80

Source: ETAS 1979, 1982 and 1988

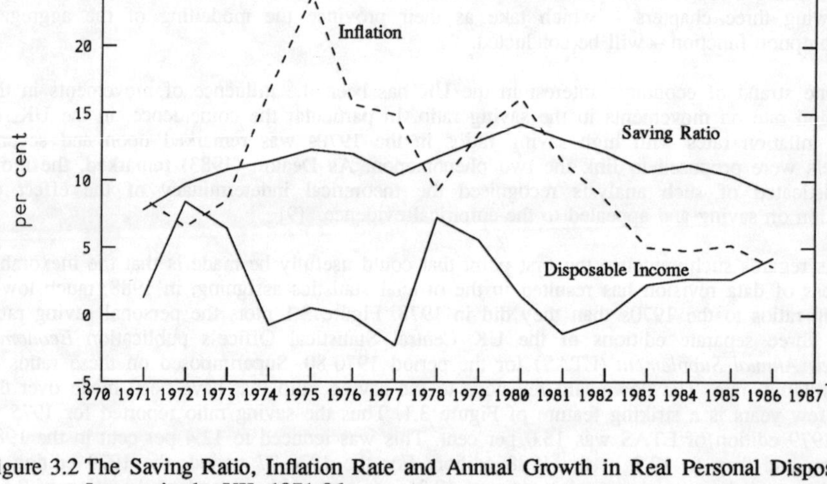

Figure 3.2 The Saving Ratio, Inflation Rate and Annual Growth in Real Personal Disposable Income in the UK, 1971-86

Source: ETAS 1988

behaviour of the saving ratio emerge from an examination of this diagram. Firstly the saving ratio tends to increase with the rate of growth of real disposable income. Secondly, there is a strong positive correlation between the saving ratio and the inflation rate. Finally there is a positive correlation between changes in the saving ratio and changes in the inflation rate.

Over the past decade four studies, each of increasing generality, have been put forward to explain movements in the UK saving ratio. [10] Against the empirical background of this section, the subsequent chapters discuss these studies and related matters in greater detail.

NOTES

[1] Known as the Stone-Geary utility function.
[2] See Chapter 2.
[3] The Hicksian demand functions are obtained by minimising the expenditure required to attain a given level of utility.
[4] Needless to say the number of budgeting stages could exceed two.
[5] In the estimation results reported in the next section, soft drinks and other manufactured food are collected together in the single category, "other manufactured food"; similarly sugar and preserves and confectionery are shown as a single category. The budget shares of the individual items in the overall group budget are shown in the tables of Appendix 3.2 to this Chapter.
[6] See Table 3.1 for a listing of these items.
[7] This imputed rent is also added to household incomings. Payments by owner-occupier households of mortgage interest are not regarded by the UKNA as part of their consumption expenditure. See Chapter 4 for a detailed discussion of the treatment of housing in the UKNA.
[8] Remembering that adding up requires the sum of the coefficients to be zero.
[9] Deaton's (1977) own model based on unanticipated inflation is discussed in Chapter 5.
[10] Deaton (1977), Davidson et al (1978), Hendry and and Pesaran and Evans (1984).

APPENDIX 3.1
Calculation of Degrees of Freedom in Consumer Demand Systems

Let n be the number of commodities in the system. The number of free parameters when *no restrictions* are imposed, with intercepts set to zero, are $(n-1)+n(n-1)=(n+1)(n-1)$ since *adding up*, which requires $\Sigma b_i=1$ and $\Sigma_i c_{ij}=0$, is automatically satisfied.
The number of free parameters when *homogeneity* only is imposed is $(n-1)+(n-1)=n(n-1)$, since now in addition $\Sigma_j c_{ij}=0$.
The number of free parameters when symmetry is imposed is $(n-1)+0.5\,(n-1)n=(n-1)(n/2+1)$.
Symmetry requires that $c_{ij}=c_{ji}$. Given that adding up $(\Sigma_j c_{ij}=0)$ is automatically satisfied, symmetry implies that homogeneity $(\Sigma_j c_{ij}=0)$ is also automatically satisfied. Therefore the number of free parameters when symmetry is imposed is $(n-1) + ((n-1)^2 + (n-1) - (n-1))/2 = (n-1) = (n-1)(n/2 + 1)$.
When *negative semidefiniteness* is imposed the number of parameters remains the same, but they are estimated subject to n inequalities.
In each case with a non-zero intercept, there are in addition $n-1$ parameters since $\Sigma a_j=0$, by adding up.

APPENDIX 3.2
Results for Testing the Restrictions of Demand Theory

Table 3.4
Testing Restrictions on the Broad Groups

$n = 11$

Null	Alternative	-2logL	df	5% Critical Value	Conclusion
HM	NR	148.06	10	18.31	Not Accepted
SY	HM	216.10	45	61.66	Not Accepted
HMSY	NR	364.16	55	73.31	Not Accepted

NR = no restrictions; HM = homogeneity; SY = symmetry; HMSY = homogeneity and symmetry; df = degrees of freedom.

Table 3.5
Testing Restrictions on Group 1 (Food)

n = 10

Null	Alternative	-2logL	df	5% Critical Value	Conclusion
HM	NR	7.76	9	16.9	Not rejected
SY	HM	67.32	36	60.0	Not accepted*
HMSY	NR	75.08	45	61.7	Not accepted*

* but not rejected at 1 per cent critical value

Table 3.6
Testing Restrictions on Group 2 (Vices)

n = 5

Null	Alternative	-2logL	df	5% Critical Value	Conclusion
HM	NR	3.42	4	9.49	Not rejected
SY	HM	4.9	6	12.60	Not rejected
HMSY	NR	8.32	10	18.30	Not rejected

Table 3.7
Testing Restrictions on Group 3 (Clothing and Footwear)

n = 3

Null	Alternative	-2logL	df	5% Critical Value	Conclusion
HM	NR	4.18	2	5.99	Not rejected
SY	HM	0.78	1	3.84	Not rejected
HMSY	NR	4.96	3	7.81	Not rejected

Table 3.8
Testing Restrictions on Group 4 (Housing)

n = 5

Null	Alternative	-2logL	df	5% Critical Value	Conclusion
HM	NR	5.84	4	9.49	Not rejected
SY	HM	10.18	6	12.6	Not rejected
HMSY	NR	16.02	10	18.3	Not rejected

Table 3.9
Testing Restrictions on Group 5 (Fuels)

n = 4

Null	Alternative	-2logL	df	5% Critical Value	Conclusion
HM	NR	19.4	3	7.81	Not accepted
SY	HM	9.36	3	17.81	Not accepted
HMSY	NR	28.76	6	12.6	Not accepted

Table 3.10
Testing Restrictions on Group 6 (Durables)

n = 5

Null	Alternative	-2logL	df	5% Critical Value	Conclusion
HM	NR	15.4	4	9.49	Not accepted
SY	HM	26.24	6	12.6	Not accepted
HMSY	NR	41.64	10	18.3	Not accepted

Table 3.11
Testing Restrictions on Group 7 (Household Goods)

n = 3

Null	Alternative	-2logL	df	5% Critical Value	Conclusion
HM	NR	4.64	2	5.99	Not rejected
SY	HM	1.64	1	3.84	Not rejected
HMSY	NR	6.28	3	7.81	Not rejected

Table 3.12
Testing Restrictions on Group 8 (Transport)

n = 7

Null	Alternative	-2logL	df	5% Critical Value	Conclusion
HM	NR	16.26	6	14.1	Not accepted*
SY	HM	22.72	20	32.7	Not Rejected
HMSY	NR	38.98	26	41.3	Not Rejected

* but not rejected at 1 per cent value

Table 3.13
Testing Restrictions on Group 9 (Communications)

n = 2

Null	Alternative	-2logL	df	5% Critical Value	Conclusion
HM	NR	3.5	1	3.84	Not Rejected

When n = 2, homogeneity implies symmetry

Table 3.14
Testing Restrictions on Group 10 (Recreational Goods & Services)

n = 8

Null	Alternative	-2logL	df	5% Critical Value	Conclusion
HM	NR	11.8	7	14.1	Not Rejected
SY	HM	44.0	21	32.7	Not accepted
HMSY	NR	56.0	28	41.3	Not accepted

Table 3.15
Testing Restrictions on Group 11 (Other Goods & Services)

n = 10

Null	Alternative	-2logL	df	5% Critical Value	Conclusion
HM	NR	39.04	9	16.9	Not Accepted
SY	HM	111.60	36	60.0	Not Accepted
HMSY	NR	150.64	45	61.7	Not Accepted

APPENDIX 3.3

Table 3.16
Expenditure and Own Price Elasticities for Group 1 (Food)

	Expenditure elasticity	Compensated price elasticity	Uncompensated price elasticity	Budget share for 1986 (%)
Bread & cereals	0.558*	-0.007	-0.084	13.73
Meat & bacon	0.792*	-0.404*	-0.608	25.69
Fish	2.038*	-1.306*	-1.380	3.58
Dairy products	0.760*	-0.151*	-0.257	13.89
Oils & fats	0.458	-0.286*	-0.309	3.30
Fruit	1.952*	-0.293*	-0.408	5.90
Beverages	1.160*	-0.215*	-0.259	3.76
Potatoes & vegetables	1.277	-0.179*	-0.333	12.01
Sugar & preserves	0.059	-0.635*	-0.642	10.63
Other manufactured food	2.766*	-0.489*	-0.696	7.51

The budget shares in Tables 3.16-3.26 are percentages of total group expenditure.

Table 3.17
Expenditure and Own Price Elasticities for Group 2 (Vices)

	Expenditure elasticity	Compensated price elasticity	Uncompensated price elasticity	Budget share for 1986 (%)
Beer	0.516*	-0.259	-0.449	36.94
Spirits	2.181*	-0.803*	-1.170	16.80
Wine, etc	1.069*	-0.548*	-0.711	15.29
Cigarettes	0.966*	-0.336	-0.598	27.09
Other tobacco	0.458	-0.052	-0.069	3.88

Table 3.18
Expenditure and Own Price Elasticities for Group 3 (Clothing and Footwear)

	Expenditure elasticity	Compensated price elasticity	Uncompensated price elasticity	Budget share for 1986 (%)
Male wear	1.210*	-0.737*	-1.076	27.99
Female wear	0.919*	-0.536*	-1.027	53.42
Footwear	0.916*	-0.458*	-0.628	18.59

Table 3.19
Expenditure and Own Price Elasticities for Group 4 (Housing)

	Expenditure elasticity	Compensated price elasticity	Uncompensated price elasticity	Budget share for 1986 (%)
Imputed rent	0.378	-0.063	-0.212	39.47
Other rent	0.395	-0.112*	-0.197	21.62
Rates etc	0.261	-0.036	-0.096	22.59
DIY goods	5.190*	-0.382	-0.841	8.82
Contractors charges etc	3.312	-1.024*	-1.272	7.50

Table 3.20
Expenditure and Own Price Elasticities for Group 5 (Fuels)

	Expenditure elasticity	Compensated price elasticity	Uncompensated price elasticity	Budget share for 1986 (%)
Electricity	0.719*	-0.154*	-0.485	46.10
Gas	0.575*	-0.116*	-0.338	38.59
Coal & coke	3.439*	-1.103*	-1.408	8.87
Other fuels	2.202*	-0.431*	-0.573	6.44

Table 3.21
Expenditure and Own Price Elasticities for Group 6 (Durables)

	Expenditure elasticity	Compensated price elasticity	Uncompensated price elasticity	Budget share for 1986 (%)
Furniture	0.591*	-1.553*	-1.662	18.38
Carpets	0.669*	-2.904*	-2.962	8.69
Household appliances	0.576*	-0.405*	-0.531	21.77
Cars etc	1.981*	-0.006	-0.609	30.45
TV radio etc	4.505	-0.260*	-0.365	20.71

Table 3.22
Expenditure and Own Price Elasticities for Group 7 (Household Goods)

	Expenditure elasticity	Compensated price elasticity	Uncompensated price elasticity	Budget share for 1986 (%)
Textiles	1.071*	-0.325	-0.638	29.23
Hardware	1.539*	-0.213	-0.875	43.05
Cleaning materials	0.088	-0.223	-0.248	27.72

Table 3.23
Expenditure and Own Price Elasticities for Group 8 (Transport)

	Expenditure elasticity	Compensated price elasticity	Uncompensated price elasticity	Budget share for 1986 (%)
Petrol	1.337*	-0.023	-0.487	34.77
Vehicle excise	0.861*	-0.029	-0.088	6.92
Other rcmv	0.983*	-0.292*	-0.543	25.57
Rail	0.392	-0.664*	-0.692	7.02
Bus	0.064	-0.894*	-0.899	8.88
Air	1.133*	-0.494*	-0.621	11.19
Other	1.136*	-0.388	-0.452	5.66

rcmv = running costs of motor vehicles

Table 3.24
Expenditure and Own Price Elasticities for Group 9 (Communications)

	Expenditure elasticity	Compensated price elasticity	Uncompensated price elasticity	Budget share for 1986 (%)
Postal services	1.243	-1.125*	-1.269	11.55
Telephones & telegraphs	0.968*	-0.147*	88.45	

Table 3.25
Expenditure and Own Price Elasticities for Group 10
(Recreational Goods and Services)

	Expenditure elasticity	Compensated price elasticity	Uncompensated price elasticity	Budget share for 1986 (%)
TV hire etc	0.908*	-0.489*	-0.595	11.62
Sports goods	1.062*	-0.892*	-0.992	9.44
Other rec goods	0.916*	-0.622*	-0.781	17.43
Betting	0.647	-1.917*	-1.985	10.50
Other rec services	0.489	-0.414*	-0.473	12.04
Books	1.231*	-0.613*	-0.657	3.59
Newspapers	0.258	-0.142*	-0.171	11.26
Expenditure abroad	1.802*	-0.639*	-1.073	24.12

Table 3.26
Expenditure and Own Price Elasticities for Group 11
(Other Goods and Services)

	Expenditure elasticity	Compensated price elasticity	Uncompensated price elasticity	Budget share for 1986 (%)
Domestic service	0.711	-0.014	-0.064	6.99
Education	0.931	-1.034*	-0.985	5.29
Chemists goods	1.432*	-0.354*	-0.411	3.94
Health	0.377	-0.322	-0.339	4.69
Toilet articles	1.039*	-0.503*	-0.585	7.89
Hairdressing	0.769	-0.779*	-0.811	4.23
Jewellery	1.581*	-1.034*	-1.115	5.12
Other goods	1.505*	-0.559*	-0.660	6.72
Catering	1.118*	-0.510*	-0.955	39.82
Other services	1.199*	-0.077	-0.260	15.31

4. Disposable resources and the consumption decision

4.1 Introduction

Over the past decade the aggregate consumption function in the United Kingdom has been the subject of intensive econometric scrutiny. [1] However all the UK studies in this area have based their work on the "conventional" United Kingdom National Accounts (UKNA) definition of personal disposable income, even though such a definition may not be the appropriate one to employ in studying consumption decisions.

The theoretical basis for applied work on the consumption function is provided by models which are hypotheses about the behaviour of individuals and households and not about institutions or businesses (cf. Keynes (1936), Friedman (1957), Ando and Modigliani (1963)) and it is the economic activity of households and individuals that are relevant to National Income determination, and to multiplier and consumption function theory. Consequently, the relevant income flow for the analysis of consumption decisions comprises factor incomes from employment, transfer incomes from other sectors and income from the ownership of capital as received by households and individuals.

Several commentators have noted that, in this respect, the UK definition of personal disposable income has not been perfect. [2] Since it is derived from the income and expenditure accounts of the personal sector it includes the incomes of private non-profit making bodies (NPMB), the property income of life assurance companies and superannuation funds (LASF), the income of unincorporated businesses (including depreciation, stock appreciation and undistributed profits) but excludes pensions and other benefits paid to households by LASF. As we shall show later in this paper, this results in values for personal disposable income and the personal saving ratio which are substantially higher than their household equivalents.

Compounding the deficiency is the fact that the UKNA accounts by following an accounting distinction between the current, capital and financial accounts leads investigators who uncritically use these accounts to make implicit, and perhaps implausible, **behavioural** assumptions about the timing of decisions. In particular the assumption implicit in all studies of the consumption function based on UKNA definitions is that current account decisions (e.g. those relating to consumption expenditure) precede capital and financial account decisions (e.g. those relating to house purchase and repayment of principal on loans).

In this context the purpose of this chapter is to first set out a detailed and consistent accounting framework for analysing household decisions. This is done in Section 2. Section 3 then uses this framework for arriving at a set of plausible assumptions about the sequencing of household decisions. Section 4 then employs this sequencing structure to firstly define appropriate measures of household income and consumption and then to construct a set of annual accounts for the household sector in the UK, for the period 1966-86. [3]

Section 5 then compares this set of households accounts with the more commonly used personal sector accounts of the UKNA paying particular attention to the distinction between "contractual" and "discretionary" saving. Section 6 then concludes the chapter.

4.2 An Accounting Framework for Households

In this section an accounting framework for analysing household behaviour is developed. This framework paves the way for the description of the measures of income appropriate for the analysis of aggregate consumption. The progressive broadening of the definition of disposable resources that has characterised recent econometric analyses of the UK consumption function (cf. Davidson et al. (1978), Hendry and Ungern-Sternberg (1981), Pesaran and Evans (1984)) reflects a growing awareness of the interconnections between stocks and flows. This subsection presents an accounting framework in which, by explicitly setting out the stock and flow accounts of the household sector, interconnections of this sort can be clearly seen. These accounts are displayed in Tables 4.1 and 4.2.

For the interpretation of these accounts it is convenient to assume initially that they relate to a single household, rather than to the sector as a whole, and that time can be adequately handled in discrete intervals of a year's duration. Thus it is supposed that a balance-sheet may be struck for the household at the end of each year with values written in under each of the headings listed in Table 4.1. The household's incomings and outgoings during the course of the following year are recorded under the headings of Table 4.2. The balance-sheet at the end of this year differs from the previous one as a consequence of transactions shown in Table 4.2, and as a consequence also of price changes and revisions in the household's expectations.

As far as possible the flows in Table 4.2 have been aligned with the stocks in Table 4.1. This is most clearly evident in the association between the assets of Table 4.1 and the current incomings in the upper panel of Table 4.2. The listing of assets in the balance-sheet derives from a life cycle perspective and consequently includes human capital. An asset is a claim on value added in the future; the balance-sheet valuation of the claim is the present discounted value of the payments expected to accrue to it. For the purposes of the present study, it will not be necessary to inquire too deeply into whose expectations are to count in the valuation of an individual household's non-marketable claims, nor into the appropriate rate of discount.

For a young household, expected future labour earnings will normally be the largest component of wealth. As the household ages, this component of wealth is amortised, with its return each year appearing as wages and salaries in Table 4.2 (incomings category 1) and the household will attempt to offset to come extent this decline in its claim on future value added by saving and building up other, non-human, components of wealth. When the household's human capital has been completely written off, at retirement, consumption in the remaining years of life must be financed entirely from payments due on, and dissaving from, the components of non-human wealth accumulated during the active years. Against the background of this life cycle perspective, the accounting structure set out in Tables 4.1 and 4.2 may be considered as a basic framework for the analysis of consumption decisions. Items

Table 4.1
Household Sector Accounts: Holdings of Asset/Liability Stocks

Assets	Liabilities
1. Human capital	1. Future tax liabilities
2. Social security wealth (gross)	2. Future national insurance contributions
3. Membership of private superannuation scheme; life assurance policies	3. Future pension scheme contributions and life assurance premiums (committed)
4. (a) Dwellings and other property	4. (a) Outstanding balance on mortgage borrowing
(b) Motor vehicles and other consumer durables	(b) Outstanding balance on other borrowing (hire-purchase debt, bank debt, other)
5. (a) Securities	
(b) Liquid assets: Notes and coin; Bank deposits; National saving	Other Net Worth
6. Claims on private trusts; Expected legacies	Pension rights, net; Housing equity; Financial assets; Other
7. (Fixed capital and stocks held in the unincorporated businesses of the self-employed).	

in the accounts are discussed now in more detail in order to establish their relationship to the appropriate measurement of income for use in the consumption function.

On the asset side of the balance-sheet, social security wealth appears "gross" (Table 4.1, asset category 2). This is the present value of the future benefit stream to which the household is entitled and expects to receive under the announced current rules of the social security system. The largest transfers within this category are state retirement pensions, included among the incomings of retired households (Table 4.2, incomings category 2). Entitlement to these benefits is supposed to be tied to the contributions made by or on behalf of households. These contributions appear among the outgoings of active households (Table 4.2, outgoings category 2) and the excess of contributions over benefits constitutes net additions to social security wealth.

Transfers from the government, which appear as incomings to households in category 2 of Table 4.2, include (among others) unemployment and sickness benefit, and supplementary and child benefit, the latter two being non-contributory. If a household were to attempt a valuation of its human capital, it would be obliged to form expectations concerning the loss of future earnings due to unanticipated periods of unemployment and sickness. The possibility of contingencies of this kind reduces human capital below what it would be otherwise. Entitlement to benefit on the occurrence of such contingencies restores some proportion of

Table 4.2
Household Sector Accounts: Income and Outlay and Transactions on Capital Account

Incomings	Outgoings
1. Wages and salaries. Income from employment paid in kind. Employers' contributions (national insurance and private).	1. Tax payments (income tax and rates)
2. Social security transfer receipts	2. National insurance contributions (employees', employers' and self-employed)
3. Private superannuation scheme pensions. Life assurance benefits.	3. Contributions to private superannuation schemes and life assurance premiums (employers', employees', and individual)
4. (a) Rent income from housing (b) Rental income from consumer durables	4. Rent payments (exclusive of heating and lighting)
5. Dividend and interest receipts	5. Interest payments on (a) mortgage (b) other debt
6. Transfers (distributed income) from private trusts. Transfers from charities and other NPMB. Transfers from abroad	6. Transfers to charities and other NPMB. Transfers abroad.
7. Self-employment income	7. Expenditure on non-durable consumption: (a) associated with income-in kind from employment (b) running costs of durables (i) maintenance (ii) insurance (iii) other (c) other (including heating and lighting)
8. Asset disposal: (a) sale of dwellings (b) sale of other consumer durables (c) sales and redemptions of financial assets (including deposit withdrawals)	8. Asset acquisition: (a) purchase of dwellings (b) purchase of motor vehicles and other consumer durables (c) purchase of financial assets (including new deposits
9. Liability acquisition: (a) new borrowing for house purchase (b) other new borrowing	9. Liability disposal: Repayments of principal on outstanding debt on (a) mortgages (b) other
10. Capital transfer receipts	10. Capital transfer payments

this wealth reduction, the exact proportion depending upon the size of the expected earnings replacement ratio.

An important lacuna in the balance-sheet of Table 4.1 is the absence of any offsetting entries for non-cash benefits expected from the government, such as education and medical care. Correspondingly there are no entries on the incomings side of Table 4.2 for the value of these services received in the current year. The omission of such entries means that the accounts are restricted to a concept of households' "private" wealth and income, augmented only by benefits provided by the government in cash, but with tax payments deducted in full. Traditionally the provision of government benefits in kind has rarely been considered an influence on households' consumption (though see Bean (1985) for an exception) and this study does not depart from the tradition.

From the standpoint of an individual household's accounts, the distinction made between gross and net social security wealth applies also to wealth held in the form of life assurance policies and membership in private superannuation schemes. Implementation of this distinction requires that the valuation for claims in asset category 3 of Table 4.1 should be taken as the present value of the future benefits receivable, rather than as the household's share in the market value of the fund's current investment portfolios. [4] When an individual first joins a pension scheme all benefits and contributions lie in the future and if the scheme is actuarially fair the valuation of the benefits will be equal to that of the contributions. As contributions are paid (Table 4.2, outgoings category 3), the liability diminishes while the benefits receivable remain unchanged (possibly increasing in the case of "with profits" policies). Consequently net worth attributable to pension rights is growing over time. In retirement, pension receipts (Table 4.2, incomings category 3) gradually reduce the valuation of pension rights.

Tangible forms of wealth appear in asset category 4 of Table 4.1 and the income generated by these assets in incomings category 4 of Table 4.2. Thus the housing services which flow from an owner-occupied dwelling are treated, conceptually, as an incoming to the home-owner, received in kind rather than cash. This income immediately reappears on the other side of the account as an imputed rent payment (Table 4.2, outgoings category 4). The effect is that expenditure on housing services is deemed to be exactly offset for owner-occupiers by their imputed rent receipts, while tenant households enjoy no such offset. Expenditure on house purchase appears in outgoings category 8(a) in the lower panel of Table 2. The value of this entry is the total cost of the house purchased by the household. For a household which is already an owner-occupier, some of the purchase price will typically be covered by proceeds from the sale of the previously owned house, shown in Table 4.2, incomings category 8(a). For first-time buyers, most of the required finance will come from the acquisition of a mortgage liability which appears in Table 4.2, incomings category 9(a). The outstanding balance of the mortgage is then entered in the balance-sheet, Table 4.1, liability category 4(a) with the housing asset entered in aset category 4(a). Analogous to the treatment of pension rights, the obligation to make mortgage payments is written down over time while the house remains on the asset side of the balance-sheet, usually gaining in value, so that the household's housing equity is growing. Mortgage payments appear in Table 4.2, split between the interest component, in outgoings category 5(a), and repayments of principal, in outgoings category 9(a). The possession of motor vehicles and other consumer durables yields services which, like housing services, may be perceived as a form of income in kind, (Table 4.2, incomings category 4(b)). Conceptually, the acquisition of consumer durables is thus treated, in an identical manner to that of house purchase, as is the treatment of debt financing for the purchase of such assets.

Wealth held in the form of financial assets appears in asset category 5 of Table 4.1 and the income generated by these assets appears as dividends and gross interest receipts in Table 4.2, incomings category 5. The use of funds to acquire financial assets appears in the lower panel of Table 4.2, outgoings category 8(c) and the source of funds realised by the disposal of such assets in incomings category 8(c). Typically, liquiid assets may be realised at their face value although for some of the deposit saving instruments included in this category, the withdrawal of funds before a stipulated redemption date entails an interest penalty. The disposal of marketable securities nearly always involves a capital gain or loss. Henceforth the difference between outgoings and incomings in category 8(c) of Table 4.2 will be referred to as "net acquisition of financial assets" in this paper. The "net disposal of financial liabilities" is the difference in the outgoings and incomings of category 9 of Table 4.2.

If a household has certain knowledge that it will receive a legacy at some date in the future, then this knowledge is likely to increase the household's perceived wealth. Expected legacies appear in Table 4.1, assets category 6. Unexpected incomings of this kind do not, of course, count, on a prior basis, as a component of wealth; when they occur, they are classic instances of "windfalls". Transfer receipts, other than from the government, are entered in Table 4.2, incomings category 6 (if they are "current"), and in incomings category 10 (if they are "capital"). The current/capital distinction makes more sense from the donor's standpoint than from the receiver's. As a donor, the household's transfer payments are entered in Table 4.2, outgoings categories 6 and 10. If, early on in life, a household forms a firm intention to leave a bequest or an estate of a certain size, or to make *intervivos* gifts of specified sizes, then the present value of the intended transfers might be regarded as a liability. However, since such bequests are voluntary (although accompanied by mandatory capital transfer tax) it is reasonable to treat them as a part of the household's net worth and hence not to record them in a separate category of the balance-sheet.

The final asset category identified in Table 4.1 related to business assets held by unincorporated enterprises owned by the household. Symmetry would require that the liabilities of such businesses, for example outstanding bank loans and trade credit, also be entered on the opposite side of the balance-sheet. In principle, the appropriate asset for inclusion in the household's balance-sheet is its claim on the future profits of the enterprise that it owns, rather than the operational assets and liabilities of the enterprise itself. But there is no general accepted method for splitting self-employment income between wages and profits and for this reason unincorporated business assets appear paranthetically in Table 4.1. As a partial adjustment, the self-employment income of households is reduced in the empirical work that follows by an allowance for the depreciation of the fixed assets held in such enterpises, and for the appreciation of stocks. This adjustment may be rationalised by the assumption that households will retain at least sufficient income to cover these items within their enterprises, rather than withdraw them for personal use. Under the same assumption, interest payments attributed to debts incurred in the course of business are also deducted from self-employment income, rather than appearing in the interest payments made by households on their own account.

Since households owning unincorporated enterprises are assessed for tax in arrears, in the UKNA it is assumed that such households set up tax reserves to cover tax payable in the following year. However these household may decide to spend the assumed net addition to tax reserves on current consumption instead of setting it aside in the form, say, of liquid assets. Following Armstrong (1979) the element of discretion is taken to be stronger here than it is in the case of depreciation and in our empirical work no deductions are made from household's incomings on account of net additions to tax reserves, which are therefore treated as being indiscriminately available to finance either current consumption or the acquisition of financial assets.

An Elaboration on Housing

Housing equity constitutes a large proportion of the household sector's net worth [5] and it is useful for an understanding of the interconnections between Tables 4.1 and 4.2 to examine the treatment of owner-occupation in somewhat more detail. Consider an active, "employee", owner-occupier household which neither receives nor makes transfer payments and which has no durable possessions other than its home. The annual cash flow balance statement for such a household may be written:

Earnings (Y1) + Dividends and interest on financial assets (Y5)

= Tax payments (E1) + Contributions (E2 + E3)

+ Mortgage interest payments (E5) + Mortgage principal

repayment (E9) + Consumers' expenditure (E7) + Net acquisition

of financial assets (E8(c)-Y8(c))

In the above identity, Y denoted an incoming, E an outgoing, and the numbers refer to the flows identified in Table 4.2. This identity takes no account of imputed rent. Suppose now that gross imputed rent is added to both sides, regarded on the left-hand side as the return to the ownership of the house, and on the right-hand side as the expenditure that the household would have been obliged to pay for the housing services it receives had it been a (private) tenant in a house of comparable quality to the one it owns (exclusive of rates which are included in E1). Deduct the mortgage interest payment (ES) from both sides of this augmented identity. The term that then appears on the left-hand side, gross rent minus mortgage interest payment, may be defined as the net rent received by the household and regarded as the return to its equity in the house that it owns.

Once the mortgage has been paid off, and provided that the house is not subsequently pledged as collateral to secure a further loan, the household's housing equity varies with the value of the house. Two asepcts of revaluation may be noted. One, usually dominant, is the general upward trend in house prices. The other, which works against the first, is the depreciation of the particular house in question – few houses, after all, endure forever. In principle, the rent charged to a private tenant household would be set sufficiently high by the landlord to cover not just the interest he must pay on any debt incurred to purchase the property, but also an allowance for depreciation, plus an element of monopoly rent. The gross rent imputed to the owner-occupier may be thought of as inclusive of all these items. However, given the general upward trend in property values, few owner-occupiers are likely to see any necessity to make provision against the distant day when their houses crumble. That day may in any case be postponed by prudent expenditure on maintenance. Such expenditure is entered as one of the running costs of durables in Table 4.2, outgoings category 7. This is cash expenditure which cannot of course be recouped from the receipts of gross rent, which are imputed. It is therefore necessary for owner-occupiers to draw upon other cash incomings if they decide to make such expenditure.

What is the point, then of augmenting the household's incomings by an imputation for gross rent which cannot be spent? The point is that the owner-occupier will indeed have more resources at his disposal than would a tenant household whose flow account was alike in all respects to the owner-occupier's, except that the gross rent entered as an outgoing was actually a cash payment with no offestting entry on the incomings side of the account. If the tenant household were to spend the same amount on maintenance as the owner-occupier, the expenditure would have to come out of a total level of disposable resources which was less than that available to the owner-occupier by the amount of the cash gross rent payment.

Maintenance expenditure has been included in the upper "current" panel of Table 4.2 primarily to accord with the traditional inclusion of such expenditure in the time series for total "consumers' expenditure" that consumption functions attempt to explain. However, to the extent that such expenditure slows down capital consumption (and thus the reduciton in wealth held in the form of housing equity due to the ageing of the housing stock) it might more appropriately be regarded as a form of saving and included in the lower "capital" panel of the Table along with house purchase in outgoings category 8(a).

4.3 The Structure and Timing of Household Decisions

This section discusses the use of the accounting structure (detailed in the previous subsection) as a framework for modelling household behaviour. The aspect of behaviour with which this chapter is primarily interested relates to aggregate consumption expenditure; however by casting the analysis within a comprehensive accounting structure the fact that the accounts embrace several items, of which consumption expenditure is but one, [6] is highlighted. Since the specific values assumed by many of these items depend upon a range of decisions made by households and since the decision of how much to spend on consumption is but one of them, it is not possible to assign values to the disposable resources available to households for consumption purposes without prior views on the timing of household decisions, these decisions being mirrored in the order in which households enter values under the headings of Table 4.2. As will be argued later in this section all analyses of the consumption function contain implicit assumptions about the sequence and timing of household decisions.

First however, using the flow chart of Table 4.3, the set of assumptions used in this paper is made explicit. The story depicted in the flow chart runs as follows. (Circles denote the times at which the indicated decisions must be taken by the household. Rectangles denote the times at which the indicated information is available to the household. All information in the rectangles preceeding a circle is therefore known to the household when it makes the circled decision, whereas none of the information in subsequent rectangles is known for certain at that time, although very good guesses might be made).

The household begins the year knowing the balance-sheet carried over from the year before. This establishes the nominal value of its initial assets and liabilities, valued with respect to stock prices determined in the previous year. At step 1, the government announces the values of the parameters of the tax and social security system to prevail during the year. These parameters include the schedule of income tax rates, levels of tax allowances, tax-exempt categories of expenditure, rate poundages for domestic property tax, national insurance contribution rates and levels of benefit. The last of these immediately establishes the value of some of the household's incomings – the amount it will receive in child benefit, for instance, if it is a household with children, or the amount it will receive as a state retirement pension if it is a pensioner household. The remaining parameters do not in themselves determine incomings and outgoings but instead define various aspects of the constraint that the household faces. If the announced parameters are significantly different from what the household had been anticipating, then it is likely that the household will consequently alter the valuation of items in its balance-sheet. More generally, each input of new information may provoke a revaluation of the balance-sheet, which should therefore be thought of as changing continually as the year progresses.

At step 2, wage rates and other terms of employment are established and, at step 3, the members of the household make their labour supply decisions. Among these decisions are the desired amounts of overtime by members already working and decisions on whether or not to search for a job, by members not working in the previous year (for example, school-leavers and housewives);and decisions to retire by the elderly members. The household discovers how well its labour supply decisions have been met at step 4, when it may find out that some members have become or remain unemployed, while others are not able to obtain as much overtime as they would wish. Thus at this step the household's annual earnings are established, and also, in conjunction with the parameters announced at step 1, the level of its national insurance contributions are determined.

The functioning of the labour market is completed by the time step 5 is reached and at this time prices are established in the remaining markets. This timing assumption allows price formation in the product markets to be based on mark-ups on unit labour costs. At step 5, the household learns what its previously determined nominal earnings are worth in terms of command over consumption goods in the current year. At the same step, the establishment of asset prices and interest rates has consequences for the determination of several items in the household's accounts. The household knows now how much interest it is committed to pay on

Table 4.3
Determination of Household Incomings and Outgoings

Steps	Incomings (Y) and Outgoings (E) determined at each step (numbers refer to Table 4.2)	
(0) Balance Sheet, end of year t-1		
(1) Government announces parameters of tax and social security system	Social security receipts (part)	Y2 (part)
(2) Wage rates established		
(3) Labour Supply		
(4) Labour Market Outcome	Income from employment	Y1
	National insurance contributions	E2
	Self-employment income	Y7
(5) Asset prices and interest rates established. House prices and rent levels established. Consumption good prices established. Parameters of private superannuation schemes and life assurance policies announced.	Private pensions and benefits	Y3
	Rent income	Y4
	Interest receipts	Y5
	Private contributions and premiums (part)	E3 (part)
	Rent payments	E4
	Interest payaments	E5
	Debt repayments	E9
(6) Mortgage Aquisition and House Purchase	New mortgage borrowing	Y9(a)
	Net house purchases	E8(a)-Y8(a)
(7) Transfers received from government	Social security receipts (remainder)	Y2 (part)
(8) Private transfers received (current and capital)	Private transfer receipts	Y6 + Y10
(9) Taxes paid (income taxes and rates)	Tax payments	E1
(10) Transfer Payments	Private transfer payments	E6 - E10
(11) Consumers' Expenditure and Net Aquisition of Financial Assets	Expenditure on non-durables	E7
	Expenditure on durables (net of sales)	E8(b)-Y8(b)
	Other new borrowing	Y9(b)
	Single Life assurance premiums	E3 (part)
	Net acquisition of financial assets	E8(c)-Y8(c)
(12) Balance Sheet, end of year t		

the outstanding debt it brought into the year, and also knows the amount of property income it would receive on its initial holdings of financial assets. Rent payments and receipts are also established at this time; cash rent payments are being treated as a prior claim on the household's resources (prior to the consumption expenditure decision made later at step 11) which a tenant household can only avoid by switching to owner-occupation. The establishment of asset prices at step 5, both for financial assets and houses, signals to the household how much its marketable assets will fetch if it decides to dispose of them in the current year – that is, capital gains and losses are ascertainable at this time. Life assurance companies and superannuation funds make use of the latest information on conditions in the financial markets to set the current parameters applicable to the financing of their schemes. As a consequence, the incomings of households in receipt of payments from the schemes are determined, and the contributions payable by household previously contracted into the schemes become known.

By the completion of step 5, the household knows most of its current incomings for the year. Its balance-sheet differs from the one it held at the beginning of the year as a result of revaluations of marketable assets, and also as a result of committed debt repayments determined at step 5. No discretionary changes in the balance-sheet have yet been made. The first opportunity to make such a change occurs at step 6, when the household may decide to buy a house or to move if it already owns one. It is being assumed that the set of decisions relating to housing, involving either a change of tenure or a change of house or both or neither, are distinct from, and in the given year, prior to the discretionary saving decision (that takes place through the medium of financial assets) at step 11. This has several implications. For an owner-occupier household not contemplating a change of residence or for a tenant household not contemplating a change of tenure it means that repayments of mortgage principal or rent payments are deducted before arriving at disposable resources; for first time buyers or for existing owner-occupiers moving house, it means that their net outlay on housing (ie. price of house less mortgage advance plus mortgage repayment) is similarly deducted.

This approach to housing decisions differs radically from their treatment in the UKNA and ipso facto from existing studies of the consumption function. In the UKNA the purchase of a new house is treated as capital formation while mortgage advances and repayments of capital are treated as part of the financial accounts analysing the use of saving. The values for saving recorded in the UKNA include house purchase expenditure and analyses of the consumption function based upon UKNA are therefore based on the implicit assumption that consumption decisions precede the house purchase decisions. This ordering of events may be mistaken for a variety of reasons. Firstly, households may reasonably regard regular repayments of mortgage principal as a committed item of expenditure that is to be deducted along with interest payments before estimating disposable income; the treatment here extends the principle of committed housing expenditure to include rent payments. Secondly, for households changing tenure and/or house in a given year, the decision to make the move may have been taken in earlier years (with an appropriate build-up in assets to say, pay for the deposit) and the observed move in a given year (ie. the implementation of decisions made earlier) may well be independent of current consumption decisions, though not, of course, of past consumption decisions. (This is more likely to be so if, as was the case in the 1970's, mortgage finance is rationed). Hence in defining the disposable resources available for consumption the net outlay on housing (capital formation in new houses less mortgage advances plus mortgage repayments) and rent is deducted from total income (cf. Armstrong (1979) for a discussion of some of these points). At step 6 the household knows the terms on which it can obtain mortgage finance, if it is able to obtain such finance at all, and it knows the prices of houses and the levels of rent.

Following the outcome of the decision made at this step, the government has enough information to determine the household's eligibility across the full spectrum of public transfer payment schemes, and these transfers are duly paid at step 7. Transfers from NPMB which in some cases may be regarded as supplements to public transfers, are received at step 8, along with transfers from abroad and from other private sector agents, including other households (for example legacies). The government now has enough information to determine the household's liability for tax in the current year and taxes are paid at step 9. At step 10 the household decided on the amount by which to deplete its own resources by making voluntary transfers to others, for example to charities or directly to other households.

Studies of aggregate consumption behaviour focus on step 11 at which time the household decides on how to allocate the resources then at its disposal (after the events and decisions earlier in the sequence) between consumption in the form of expenditure on goods and services and saving in the form of financial assets. The outcome of the housing decision at step 6 is very likely to affect the household's net acquisition of financial assets since if it does purchase a house then it is likely to dispose of some of its financial assets to cover the down payment. On the other hand it is not likely that there will be much effect in the reverse direction within the current year. Of course the outcome of the consumption/saving decision (at step 11) influences the balance-sheet that the household carries forward and hence affects the house purchase decision in subsequent years.

At the stage of determining its consumption expenditure a household could decide to augment its resources by borrowing in order to finance its consumption. In a complete model, this decision may occur simultaneously with the consumption decision, so that consumers' expenditure, particularly on durable and semi-durable goods, would depend (among other factors) upon the amount of borrowing, while at the same time, the extent of the household's borrowing would depend upon the availability and the conditions of credit as well as upon its expenditure on durable and semi-durable goods. An analysis of the borrowing decision is outside the scope of this book and it is therefore assumed that the consumer reaches step 11 with a level of disposable resources which it augments with new borrowings and then makes the consumption/saving decision on the basis of these augmented resources. [7] The household may also augment resources by selling financial assets and it is at this time that the capital gains or losses ascertained at step 5 may be realised. The outcome of the group of decisions taken at step 11 completes the determination of the entries in the household's accounts. The assets and liabilities of Table 4.1 are then carried forward by the incomings and outgoings of Table 4.2 to form, with the appropriate revaluations included, the initial balance-sheets for the following year. Again the story told in this chapter differs from the more conventional, UKNA based story in the treatment of consumer credit. In the UKNA, consumer credit and capital repayments of such credit are part of the financial accounts and hence do not determine the volume of saving. In this chapter repayments of principal, as a committed payment, reduce disposable resources and new borrowings augment such resources. Consequently both items affect household saving.

To summarise, the view of the consumption decision put forward here is that it is conditional upon the household's labour, investment and transfer income; it is also conditional on the cost of housing services, which is treated as a prior claim on resources; it is conditional as well as upon the house purchase decision which, in a given year, is assumed to be prior to the consumption decision; finally it is conditional on new borrowing for consumption purposes less repayments on past borrowings.

In casting the analysis within the accounting framework outlined above the concept of saving alters from the UKNA construct. In the UKNA the double entered flow "saving", which is used to make the transition from the current to the capital account, is an accounting construct for which there is no actual transaction that households undertake. In the concept employed in this chapter, when households reach the consumption decision, they are not deciding how much of their income to carry into their capital account; rather they are deciding on the allocation of resources, still left at their disposal after prior commitments have been discharged and prior decisions have been made, between the two markets for consumption goods and financial assets.

Thus under this concept, a distinction emerges, between committed and discretionary saving with the consumption decision influencing the latter but not the former. Committed saving consist of all the regular payments, resulting from previously entered contracts, that serve to increase household equity in a variety of assets (eg. equity in housing, pension funds). It is the contention of this paper that this concept of saving accords better with existing institutional arrangements than the more conventional concept, where, with all saving regarded as discretionary, a far greater degree of choice is assigned to households than their existing contracts and commitments would lead them to possess. With these observations, the next section turns to a discussion of the data used to instill empirical content into these ideas.

4.4 The Construction of Household Sector Accounts

Data on the household sector's (including private trusts) current account has been available in the UKNA tables on an annual basis since 1966 and the econometric revaluation of the UK consumption function (presented in the next chapter) is based on this data for the period 1966-86. In this section the data used in the econometric work are described and an attempt is also made to interpret the data within the framework set out earlier and to contrast this with some alternative interpretations.

Most of the relevant magnitudes for the illustrative year, 1986, are displayed in Table 4.4. The division between parts A and B of this table is meant to correspond to a line drawn in Table 4.3 immediately before step 11. Thus the cumulative algebraic sum of all the items in parts A and B of the table indicates the composition of the disposable resources with which households, in aggregate, entered the product and financial asset markets in 1986; the figures in part B show the outcome of the allocation of these resources between these two markets. However, there are several important qualifications to this statement which are brought out in the following discussion. Many of the necessary qualifications stem from the fact that the recent UKNA presentation of the household sector's accounts, as distinct from the personal sector's, has not yet been extended to the capital account. As a consequence a number of assumptions with regard to the allocation of items in the personal sector's capital account have had to be made and these are discussed first.

For individual households, it is very likely that the bulk of the capital transfers received and paid in any year are between households (or to households from the estates of households). When the accounts of households are consolidated, such transfers disappear. What remains are primarily transfers to and from the government and to and from NPMB. In Table 4.4, line 15, only one flow has been entered: total capital taxes paid by the personal sector. Nearly half of this flow is made up of death duties, which are clearly incident on households, while the remainder is mainly capital gains tax, some of which may be paid by unincorporated businesses within the household sector. However it is reasonable to suppose that capital gains tax paid by such enterprises are a charge against that portion of self-employed income which has been assumed to accrue to the households owning the enterprises, and thus reasonable to deduct it in Table 4.4. Most of the capital transfers paid by the government to the personal sector are known to flow to NPMB, such as universities. Some of such transfers flow to households, for example home improvement grants, but these items are not separately identified in the UKNA capital accounts. Similarly it is not possible to identify capital transfers between households and NPMB, such as, for example, bequests to charities.

As discussed in the previous section, expenditure on house purchase is deducted (at line 17) in part A of Table 4.4. If all purchases of land and dwellings by households were from other households, this figure, upon consolidation, would sum to zero, except for the cost of transfer fees. It differs from zero for two reasons: purchase of newly constructed houses, and purchases (less sales) of land and existing houses from other sectors. The latter component has been large and positive in recent years as a result of the purchase by tenant households of council houses. In the earlier years of the period, this component was frequently negative, reflecting, for example, the sale of land by farmers for development purposes, or the sale of dilapidated houses to local authorities under slum clearance programmes. The total entered at line 17 relates to the personal sector as a whole and therefore includes an element of capital formation in dwellings by housing associations, which are classified as NMPB. However this

Table 4.4
Sources and Uses of Funds: Household Sector 1986

A	Components of "Disposable Resources"	£ million	Entries in Table 4.2
1	Wages and salaries	179,183	
2	+Income in kind	3,396	Y1
3	+Employers' contributions(i)	26,866	
4	+Social security receipts	40,616	Y2
5	+Private pensions and benefits	23,775	Y3
6	+Rent, dividends, and interest(ii)	34,520	Y4+Y5
7	+Other current transfers	9,638	Y6
8	+Self-employment income (iii)	28,679	Y7
	Total Income	346,673	
9	-Tax payments: income tax(iv)(v)	44,058	
	rates(vi)	8,033	E1
10	-National insurance contributions(vii)	25,784	E2
11	-Private contributions and premiums(part) (v)(viii)	26,660	E3(part)
12	-Rent payments: imputed on owner-occupation	13,610	
	other(vi)	7,489	E4
13	-Interest payments	17,717	E5
14	-Current transfer payments	3,749	E6
15	-Net capital transfer payments(ix)	1,927	E10-Y10
16	+Net borrowing for house purchase(x)	25,503	Y9(a)-E9(a)
17	-Net expenditure on house purchase	14,823	E8(a)-Y8(a)
18	+Other net borrowing (consumer credit)(xii)	4,552	Y9(b)-E9(b)
	"Disposable Resources"	212,878	
B	Uses of "Disposable Resources"		
19	Expenditure on non-durables	170,938	E7
20	Expenditure on durables (xiii)	23,582	E8(b)-Y8(b)
21	Total "Consumption Expenditure"(xiv)	194,520	
22	Single life assurance premiums(xv)	5,350	E3(part)
23	"Net acquisition of financial assets"(xvi)	13,008	E8(c)-Y8(c)
24	Total "saving" (lines 22+23)	18,358	

Source: UKNA 1987.

Notes to Table 4.4

All figures are from UKNA 1987, Table 4.9, except as noted below.

(i)	Employers' contributions: UKNA 1987 Table 4.1	National insurance Other	13,257 13,609

(ii) Including imputed rent of owner-occupied dwellings (UKNA 1987 Table 4.1), deducted at line 12.

(iii) After deducting allowances for depreciation and stock appreciation and excluding interest payments attributed to business debt.

(iv) Excluding net additions to tax reserves.

(v) Premium outgoings attract tax relief. From 1979, the method of granting relief is that households pay premiums to life funds net of tax and consequently are assessed for tax on their taxable incomes before the deduction of premiums. The central government compensates life funds for the shortfall in premiums due to tax relief (amount shown in UKNA 1987 Table 4.10). In Table 4.4 above, premiums are shown gross and household recorded tax payments are reduced by the amount of tax relief.

(vi) Rates, sewerage and water charges Other (non-imputed) rent payments UKNA 1987 Table 4.7

(vii) National insurance contributions: Employers' 13,257(as note (i))
Employees' 12,527

(viii)	Private contributions:	Employers'	13,609(as note(i))	
		Employees'	5,062	
		Regular individual premiums for life policies	7,989	(UKNA 1987 Table 4.5)

(ix) Capital taxes paid by the personal sector, UKNA 1987 Table 4.2.

(x) Financial Statistics, December 1987, Table 6.3.

(xi) Gross domestic fixed capital formulation of personal sector
in dwellings 11,220
purchases less sales of land and existing buildings 3,603
(UKNA 1987 Table 4.2) (personal sector here excludes LASF but includes NPMB and unincorporated businesses)

(xii) Financial Statistics, December 1987, Table 9.3.

(xiii) UKNA 1987 Table 4.5.

(xiv) UKNA 1987 Table 4.4, less rates and other rent payments shown in lines 9 and 12.

(xv) UKNA 1987 Table 4.10.

(xvi) Computed as residual; therefore it includes all unidentified items as well as actual transactions in the listed financial assets of Table 4.1.

element is not likely to be large in comparison with purchases by households.

For reasons indicated in the previous section net borrowing for house purchase (new mortgage advances less principal repayments on existing mortgages) is also included in part A of Table 4.4. In fact, the transactions on capital account associated with house purchase are actually a net source of funds for the household sector as a whole (line 16-line 17). This fact was noted by Armstrong (1979) and has been further analysed by Davis and Saville (1982), but is concealed in conventional analyses of consumption behaviour. [8] It is worth pausing to consider how it can happen that housing capital transactions are able to provide households (in aggregate) with an additional source of funds that may then be spent on consumption or the acquisition of other types of asset. One way this may happen is through the operation of housing chains. As a stylised example, consider four households. Household H4 comprises of a retired couple (or widow) which has decided, all children having departed, to sell the family home, worth 30 and owned outright, and to buy a smaller retirement dwelling worth 10, which has just been constructed. Household H3 which buys the house from H4 for 30, has "traded up" the housing ladder and has sold a house worth 20 and taken out a new mortgage for 10 to cover the difference. Similarly, moving into H3's old house is household H2 which has sold a home worth 10 and taken out a mortgage for 10. At the end of the chain is H1, a newly formed household or a former tenant household, which buys H2's old house for 10 and to do so takes out a mortgage for the full amount. the total amount of mortgage finance raised by the four households is 30. Their total net expenditure on housing is 10, the value of the newly built house purchased by H4. In this example the difference of 20 accrues entirely to the benefit of household H4, which has thereby realised some of its housing equity.

A further reason why net mortgage advances can exceed expenditure on houses is that some of the borrowing under this heading may be obtained for the purpose of home improvements by owner-occupiers and such expenditure is not included in the UKNA capital account (unless it is grant-aided) but rather as a component of consumers' expenditure. Improvements are thus classified together with maintenance expenditure as consumption, although conceptually, as noted earlier, this type of expenditure might be regarded as a form of saving since it builds up, or retards the depreciation of, housing equity. In 1986, a little under 4 per cent of the total expenditure on non-durables shown in Table 4.4 was spent in this way. The treatment of the other items in Table 4.4 is fairly uncontentious with a few exceptions. On the composition of consumers' expenditure, it should be pointed out that the figure shown in Table 4.4 excludes rent and rates. Our focus is on the behaviour of households with regard to the fraction of their discretionary cash incomings that they decide to save. Rent and rates are prior claims on these incomings, and thus committed expenditure over which households have little choice (other than to go into arrears) and therefore do not feature in this decision. To some extent, expenditure on fuel and power (just over 10 per cent of non-durable expenditure) falls into the same category; however households may choose to conserve on the consumption of fuel and power, just as car-owning households have the option of varying the running costs of their cars.

Another difficult item is other net borrowing in line 18. The location of this item on a net basis in part A of the table masks its treatment in Table 4.3 of the previous section. In the previous table, repayments of debt were treated as being determined prior to step 11 in the decision sequence. New borrowing was then shown as being determined at step 11 together with the level of expenditure on durables. For consistency with this previous treatment, repayments of other debt should be included (negatively) in part A of Table 4.4, as a form of committed expenditure, while new borrowing should be included (negatively) in part B as an additional discretionary source of "cash". However the data source does not permit the complete decomposition of the net figure into its two gross components. Consumer borrowing from retailers and finance houses is available on a gross basis, but borrowing from banks only on a net basis. In our empirical work we have therefore employed the treatment as in Table 4.4 where net borrowing augments existing disposable resources.

A rationalisation of this treatment of consumer credit, might be made in terms of liquidity constraints; Stibbard (1979), in introducing the CSO's new consumer credit series, drew attention to a peak in the proportion of expenditure on durables covered by net consumer credit in the earlier 1970's when hire purchase controls were relaxed. At the same time, as shown in Calder (1978), there was a notable increase in expenditure on durables. This association suggests that a large number of households are liquidity-constrained and that the availability of retail finance is, to a large degree, an exogenously determined variable as far as households' expenditure plans are concerned. However the proper treatment of this issue required that expenditure on durables and the related debt finance be considered within a simultaneous equation framework (cf. Garganas (1975), Borooah (1978) for such studies).

Non-availability of gross figures also prevents the treatment of save as you earn (SAYE) saving using the predetermined and committed versus discretionary analysis of section 4.2.

According to this analysis, once a SAYE scheme has been entered, all subsequent regular payments become committed; it is only the initial deposit that is discretionary in any year (cf. Toland (1981)). When the contracted duration of the SAYE plan is complete, the accumulated funds may be withdrawn together with the bonus interest payment that distinguishes such plans. To carry this logic through to Table 4.4, regular SAYE deposits less non-penalised withdrawals should be deducted in part A, as well as from the net acquisition of financial assets in part B, leaving only the initial deposits as a component of discretionary saving. Toland (1981) includes among SAYE plans the subscription shares offered by building societies, but unfortunately only the net payments into such shares are available for recent years. There was a surge in such shares in 1981 and it is impossible to tell from the data whether it was due to a large inflow of new initial deposits or to a temporary reduction in withdrawals from accounts previously established. No adjustments has been made for this form of saving which is therefore being treated on a net basis as a form of discretionary saving (line 23, Table 4.4).

With these caveats, and adopting the treatment of other borrowing illustrated in Table 4.4, it appears that households, in aggregate, decided to allocate 6 per cent of their discretionary cash incomings in 1986 to the net acquisition of financial assets. In principle, of course, the net acquisition of financial assets in any year could be negative (although this is unlikely for the sector as a whole). Discretionary cash incomings, in the sense of the sum of the items shown in part A of Table 4.4, are only part of the disposable resources of the household sector; households are also able to sell assets, the cash proceeds of which appear as negative saving in part B of the table. In the empirical attempt to explain saving behaviour, the magnitude of the household sector's initial assets available for disposal is treated as a separate explanatory variable, as are the capital gains attributable to these assets as a result of the functioning of the assets market during the current year.

4.5 A Comparison of Household and Personal Sector Accounts

The magnitude of the adjustments, detailed in the previous section for the illustrative year 1986, are shown in Table 4.5 for each year of the period 1976-86. These are the household income and expenditure accounts. Set alongside them on the left-hand side of Table 4.5 are the values for the personal sector's disposable income, consumption and saving, for the same period, as reported in the UKNA accounts. These latter figures relating to the personal sector, form the basis for most econometric studies of the consumption function. The right-hand side of Table 4.5 isolates the household component of the personal sector and reports values for household disposable resources, consumption and saving consistent with the treatment outlined in section 4.4. Figure 4.1 then shows household disposable resources (income), consumption and saving as percentages of the respective personal sector values. Over the period 1976-86, the average reductions, as a result of isolating the household sector and of making the adjustments described above, were 20.2, 15.8, and 52.8 per cent for income, consumption and saving respectively. The percentage reduction in disposable resources (income) shows markedly more variation than the percentage reduction in consumption and this has a considerable impact on discretionary household saving as a percentage of personal saving.

The two saving ratios are plotted in Figure 4.2 with the top line representing the personal saving ratio (ie. personal saving as a percentage of personal disposable income) and the bottom line representing the household saving ratio (ie. household discretionary saving as a percentage of household disposable resources). On average, over 1976-86, households saved just under 7 per cent of their disposable resources, after their prior commitments had been met and their prior decisions had been implemented and this contrasts with an average personal sector saving ratio, over the same period, of just under 12 per cent. Movements in the two ratios, over the period 1976-86, has however been in opposite directions; the household saving ratio has shown a broadly upward trend while the personal saving ratio has, if anything, tended to fall. As a consequence the average gap between the two ratios over the 5 year period 1982-86 has narrowed to 3.1 percentage points in contrast to an average difference over the entire period, 1976-86, of 4.9 percentage points. The clue to these

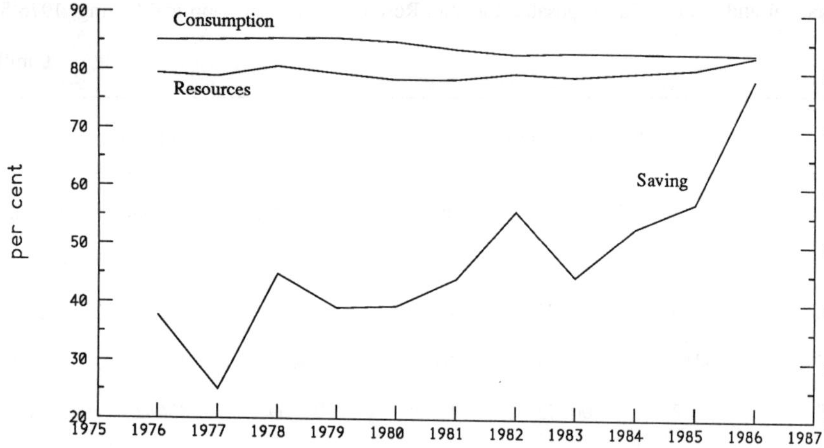

Figure 4.1 Household Disposable Resources, Consumption and Saving as a Percentage of Corresponding Personal Sector Values

Source: UKNA and own calculations

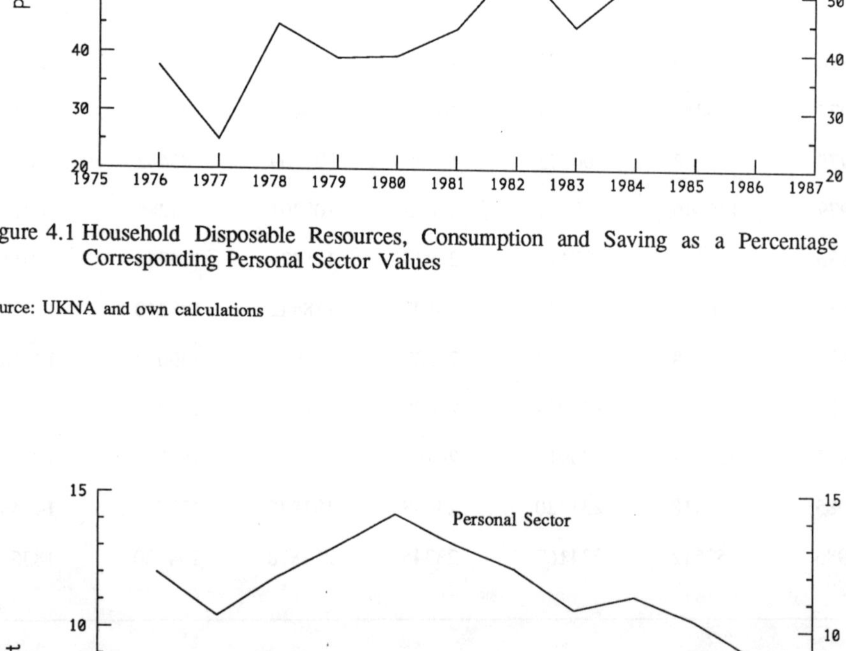

Figure 4.2 Personal and Household Saving as a Percentage of their Respective Disposable Incomes

Source: UKNA and own calculations

Table 4.5
Personal and Household Disposable Income, Resources, Consumption and Saving, 1976-86.

£ million

	Personal Sector			Households		
	Disposable Income	Consumption	Saving	Disposable Resources	Consumption	Saving (discretionary)
1976	86229	75873	10356	68490	64584	3906
1977	96862	86757	10105	76484	73958	2526
1978	113462	100023	13439	91509	85482	6027
1979	136046	118361	17685	108201	101286	6915
1980	160297	137470	22827	125879	116868	9011
1981	176132	153027	23105	138442	128240	10202
1982	190938	167599	23339	152047	139017	13030
1983	205096	183068	22028	162255	152437	9818
1984	220711	195912	24799	176151	163007	13144
1985	238418	231720	24698	191845	177702	14143
1986	257512	234167	23345	212878	194520	18358

Source: UKNA 1987

movements is provided in Figure 4.1. This shows that, "household" consumption expenditure as a percentage of "personal sector" consumption expenditure is about 2 percentage points less in the period 1982-86 as compared to 1976-80. At the same time, disposable household resources as a percentage of personal disposable income has remained fairly stable.

The essential difference between the consumption expenditure of households and the personal sector is that, on our definition, household expenditure excludes final expenditure by NPMB, the administrative costs of LASF and rates and rent payments. Consumers' expenditure of the personal sector, as defined in the UKNA, includes these items but, additionally, excludes expenditure by foreign tourists in the UK. Over the period 1976-86, while aggregate personal sector consumers' expenditure in current prices grew at an average annual rate of 12 per cent, expenditure by households on rates and rent, final expenditure by NPMB and the administrative costs of LASF grew, respectively, at 13, 14 and 17 per cent per annum. Indeed this disparity between the aggregate growth rate and the growth rate of the second and the third of the above components was even more marked over the years 1982-86, during which the relevant annual growth rates in the components of expenditure, noted above were 9, 14 and 16 per cent respectively. Thus the major reason, since 1982, for the narrowing

Table 4.6
The Composition of Household Saving, 1976-86

£ million

	Discretionary	Committed		Total Committed	Total Saving
		LASF contributions	Mortgage repayments		
1976	3906	5322	966	6288	10194
1977	2526	6393	1209	7602	10128
1978	6027	7704	1576	9280	15307
1979	6915	10085	1446	11531	18446
1980	9011	12050	1434	13484	22495
1981	10202	13612	1926	15538	25740
1982	13030	13904	2958	16862	29892
1983	9818	14188	3466	17654	17472
1984	13144	15525	3056	18581	31725
1985	14143	15762	3902	19664	33807
1986	18358	14760	4663	19423	37781

Sources: UKNA 1987 and Financial Statistics.

of the gap between the saving ratio of the personal sector and that of households has been the relatively faster growth in the components of expenditure which are excluded from the household accounts but included in the personal sectors' accounts, viz. expenditure on rents and rates by households, NPMB final expenditure and LASF administrative costs.

The composition of household saving is set out in Table 4.6. The broad distinction made with regard to its composition is between committed and discretionary saving. note 1 discretionary saving. Within the category of committed saving, two components – life assurance and pension fund contributions and repayments on mortgage principal – are distinguished; they serve to increase equity in pension funds and dwellings respectively. Repayments of principal on consumer credit, which increase equity in durable consumer goods, are not treated as a component of contractual saving, and the UKNA convention of regarding expenditure on such goods as a part of consumption is followed. Only regular repayments on mortgage principal are regarded as committed saving; [9] early repayments of principal are regarded as a discretionary decision, though it is a discretion exercised in the housing decision which is, as noted earlier, assumed to be prior to, and distinct from, the consumption decision.

Contractual saving through pension funds is regarded as the increase in net pension fund wealth and is defined as the excess of the sum of the contributions to such funds and the investment income of these funds over the pensions and benefits paid and the administrative expenses incurred by the funds. [10] This interpretation of contractual saving by households in life assurance and pension fund schemes is different from the interpretation adopted by Armstrong (1979) and Cuthbertson (1982) who regard only employees' contributions as falling under this contractual category. This latter interpretation however ignores the fact that households, who contribute to such schemes, may be aware that contributions are also being made on their behalf by their employers; if, at the same time, ownership of such funds is to be assigned to households (although the funds may be managed by others) then any increase in such funds must be part of households saving.

As can be seen from Table 4.6 the bulk of saving is either discretionary, through the purchase of financial assets, or committed through life assurance companies and pension funds with, in the last 3 years, the former being dominated by the latter for each year of the period 1976-85. On the definition of saving adopted in this chapter, households, by acquiring either financial assets or equity in pension funds and dwellings, "saved", in 1986, a total of £37,781 million, of which almost half represented "discretionary" saving. This contrasts with the conventional national accounts definition which regards saving as a purely current account transaction defined as simply the excess of current disposable income over current consumption expenditure where the latter excludes expenditure on the purchase of dwellings but includes expenditure on consumer durables. Thus on this definition, personal sector saving, as reported in the UKNA, was, in 1986 at £23,345 million only 62 per cent of the value (reported above) for total household saving.

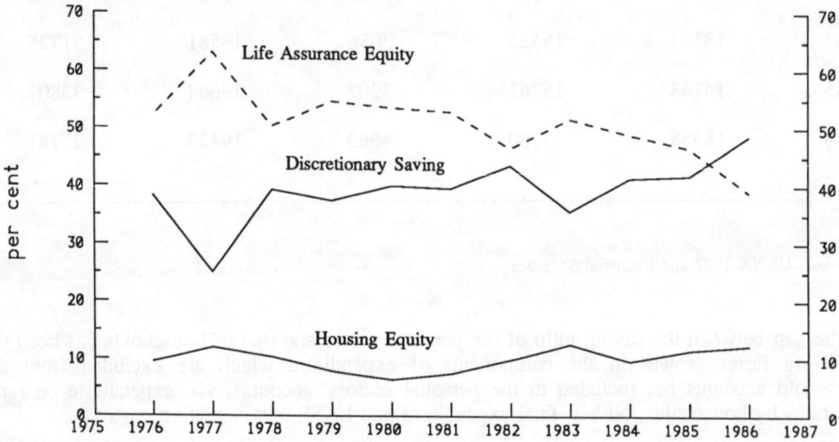

Figure 4.3 The Components of Household Saving as a Proportion of Total Saving

Source: own calculations

The percentage contributions of discretionary saving, saving through the acquisition of pension fund equity and saving through the acquisition of equity in dwellings are illustrated in Figure 4.3. As can be readily seen households, in the main, save by either acquiring financial assets or pension fund equity. Over the period 1986-86, on average 50 per cent of household saving was through acquiring pension fund equity, 40 per cent through acquiring financial assets and only 10 per cent through the acquisition of equity in dwellings. This picture has however changed quite considerable in the past few years and over the period 1982-86, the share of discretionary saving in total saving rose to 42 per cent while that of pension fund equity acquisitions fell to 47 per cent.

4.6 Concluding Remarks

The argument of this chapter has been that the definition of personal disposable income adopted in the UK national accounts might not be the appropriate one to employ for the study of consumption decisions. This was for essentially two reasons. First, because the personal sector, contained a non-household component in the form of unincorporated businesses, non-profit making bodies and life assurance companies and pension funds and second because the use of the national accounts definition involved making implicit, and perhaps implausible, assumptions about the timing of household decisions.

To rectify this, the chapter began by investigating the structure of household decisions in terms of the components of its balance sheet of assets and liabilities, in terms of changes to these components and in terms of the sequencing in time of such changes. This exercise then enabled one to see firstly, that the consumption decision was one of a myriad of decisions taken by households and secondly that in the timing of such decisions it could plausibly be regarded as occupying a certain position in relation to the other decisions. Furthermore, this position then determined the available resources, in the context of which these consumption decisions were then to be made. These conceptual issues were made more concrete by the construction of a consistent set of household accounts for the UK which embodied these ideas. Differences over the past 11 years between the income, consumption and saving experience of the personal sector and the household sector in the UK were then explored using these accounts. The next chapter attempts an econometric revaluation of the consumption function in the UK using the ideas developed here.

NOTES

[1] See for example Hendry (1974), Ball et al. (1975), Wall et al. (1975), Deaton (1977), Davidson et al. (1978), Hendry and Ungern-Sternberg (1981), Ungern-Sternberg (1981), Davidson and Hendry (1981), Davis (1982), Deaton (1983), Hendry (1983), Hendry (1983), Muellbauer (1983) and Pesaran and Evans (1984).

[2] See for example Moyle and Reid (1975), Royal Commission on the Distribution of Income and Wealth (1975), Borooah (1978), Stark (1978) and Jones (1981).

[3] This construction has been made possible by the very considerable efforts that the Central Statistical Office has put into providing time series data on the incomes and expenditures of households (cf. Moyle and Reid (1975), Stibbard (1979), Jones (1981), and Toland (1981)).

[4] Indeed many private schemes (inclusive of those run for public sector employees) do not have accumulated funds which can be valued in the market. In 1980, 34.9 per cent of the payments in incomings category 3 of Table 4.2 were made from unfunded and nationally funded schemes while 31.2 per cent of contributions were made to such schemes.

[5] There are no estimates of this proportion conceptually congruent to the headings of Table 4.1. Nevertheless the importance of housing equity is readily apparent in the personal sector's balance sheets drawn up on CSO definitions. At the end of 1980 the percentage composition of net worth was estimated to be:

Housing equity	39.6
Equity in insurance and pension funds (market valuation)	13.7
Other	46.7

[6] Table 4.2, outgoings categories 7 and 8(b).

[7] The new borrowing of course leads to increased financial liabilities which in turn lead to increased future repayments of principal and interest.

[8] This fact was noted also in *The Economist*, 28 April 1984, with reference to bank of England estimates of the "massive" rate at which the personal sector is withdrawing equity from the housing market.

[9] Data on regular repayments is only available for building societies; all repayments on mortgage principal to local authorities and insurance companies are regarded as committed saving.

[10] See the discussion in section 4.2.

5. The consumption function in the UK: A revaluation

5.1 Introduction

The previous chapter developed the concept of a household's "disposable resources" based on an explicit consideration of the structure and sequencing of household decisions. It was argued in that chapter that such a concept of disposable resources was perhaps more appropriate for the study of household consumption decisions than the concept of personal disposable income used in the United Kingdom National Accounts (UKNA). However it was also noted in that chapter that although the consumption function in the United Kingdom had, over the past decade, been the subject of intensive econometric scrutiny, such scrutiny had been within the context of the "conventional" (and as was argued, perhaps inappropriate) definitions of consumers' expenditure and disposable income employed by the UKNA. The purpose of this chapter is to rectify this shortcoming in the UK consumption function literature. This it attempts to do by considering the four major versions of the consumption function put forward for the UK in the past ten years and reappraising these in the light of the concepts developed in the previous chapter.

These four major models of the aggregate consumption-income relationship in the UK are those of Deaton (1977), Davidson et al. (1978), Hendry and Ungern-Sternberg, and Pesaran and Evans (1984). The next section provides a brief exposition of these models paying careful attention to their essential differences and similarities. The section following that, investigates the empirical properties of these models when they were re-estimated within the conceptual framework of the previous chapter. Since in their original estimated form, these models differed with respect to the definition of consumers' expenditure adopted for explanation, the estimation period and the frequency of the data observations, [1] the first problem, was to reduce them to a common form. Given that data on household income and expenditure was available only in annual form, only annual analogues of these models could be considered. The periods 1955-86 and 1966-86 were adopted as the common estimation periods and the models were formulated so as to explain the totality of consumers' expenditure but with attention paid as well to the non-durable component of such expenditure.

The sequencing of the comparisons was as follows: first, the models were estimated on annual data over the period 1955-86, using UKNA definitions of disposable income and consumers' expenditure, with the focus being on total consumers' expenditure. These results, shown in the first row of Tables 5.1 -5.4, were then compared with the original results, to see whether the specifications were robust in the face of changes in the estimation period, frequency of observation and definitions of consumers' expenditure. The answer invariably was that they were. The equations were then re-estimated over the period 1966-86, to see whether simply altering the estimation period influenced the results, and the results of this alteration are shown as the second row of Tables 5.1-5.4. Finally, the equations were estimated over 1966-86, but this time using the household "disposable resources" and consumers' expenditure concepts developed in the previous chapter and these results are shown in the last row of Tables 5.1-5.4. By doing so, it was intended, that the final step would isolate the marginal contribution, of the changed concepts, to the results.

5.2 The Consumption Function in the UK: a review of four models

Consumers' Expenditure and Unanticipated Inflation, Deaton (1977)

In the 1970s a great deal of research effort in both the UK and the USA was directed towards an understanding of whether there was a causal link between the high inflation rates and the high saving ratios that prevailed over much of the decade. [2] Prominent among models that sought to establish the existence of such a link was that of Deaton (1977). He argued that, typically purchases were made sequentially, so that while the purchaser had precise and up-to-date information about the prices of commodities actually being bought, his information about the prices of commodities bought at an earlier point in time, would tend to be outdated. As a consequence consumers had no means of distinguishing between relative price changes and absolute price changes.

This problem would be particularly acute when inflation was not correctly anticipated, for, in such a situation, consumers would mistake a general change in prices for a relative change in the prices of commodities bought by them. Thus, by way of example, if the rate of increase in prices expected by the consumer, since his last shopping trip, was 1 per cent, but the true increase was 2 per cent then his observation that coffee was now 2 per cent more expensive than last time, would cause him to conclude that the price of coffee had gone up relative to the prices of other commodities and thus lead him to buy less of it. Since a similar situation would face all other consumers, there would be a mass illusion that all goods were relatively more expensive, causing aggregate consumption to fall and the saving ratio to rise. In other words, in a period where consumers underestimated the time rate of price increase, there would be a positive relation between the inflation rate and the saving ratio.

In order to test this hypothesis for the UK Deaton (1977) estimated an equation of the form:

$$S_t = \alpha_0 + \alpha_1 g_t + \alpha_2 \pi_t + \alpha_3 S_{t-1} + v_t \qquad (5.1)$$

where S is the saving ratio; g is the rate of growth of real disposable income; π is the inflation rate, defined as the rate of increase in p, the consumers price deflator; v is an error term and t is the time subscript.

Equation (5.1) incorporates a partial adjustment mechanism, within a permanent income framework, and combines this with an unanticipated inflation effect, the latter being proxied by the actual inflation rate. Estimation of this equation on data for the UK (over the period 1955 Q3 – 1974 Q3) and for the USA (over the period 1954 Q2 – 1974 Q2) showed that although the estimates of the growth rate parameter (α_1) differed between the countries, the estimates of the inflation and adjustment rate parameters (respectively α_2 and α_3) were very similar. These showed that, in both countries, when the quarterly rate of inflation was running at 2 per cent above the anticipated rate, slightly more than 1 per cent of disposable income was saved involuntarily.

Consumers' Expenditure and the Error Correction Mechanism, Davidson et al. (1978)

The next major study of aggregate consumption behaviour in the UK was that of Davidson et al. (1978). The motivation for their study was the observation that, despite the plethora of econometric investigations into the relationship between consumers' expenditure and disposable income in the UK, no consensus had emerged regarding the short run dynamics between these two variables. The correct specification of the dynamics of the consumption/disposable income relation was therefore the primary aim of the their study. They hoped to achieve this in the context of "best practice" modelling which, in their view, was enshrined in three principles.

Firstly, Davidson et al. (1978) enunciated the very important principle of "encompassing", by which existing models were only supplanted by a new model, if the latter could be shown to be capable of accounting for the findings of the former. The second principle was that of "theory consistency" – the new model was only admissible if it was conceived within a theoretical framework. Finally, the third principle was one of "data coherency" – the new model at the very minimum should satisfactorily "fit" the data that it purported to explain, both in terms of its "historical" values, on which the model was estimated, and in terms of its "future" values, which the model could forecast. [3]

Within this general framework, the starting point of the Davidson et al. (1978) model was a general dynamic relation between real consumers' expenditure on non-durable goods and services, cnd, and real disposable income y with inflation effects *a la* Deaton (1977) included so that

$$\alpha(L)\log cnd_t = k + \beta(L)\log y_t + \theta_1\pi_t + \theta_2\Delta\pi_t + v_t \tag{5.2}$$

where Δ is the first difference operator; $\alpha(L)$ and $\beta(L)$ are polynomials in the lag operator, L; k is the intercept, and v is an error term.

If it is assumed that $\alpha(L)$ and $\beta(L)$ are of the first order, one obtains:

$$\Delta\log cnd_t = k + \beta_1\Delta\log y_t + (\beta_1 + \beta_2)\log y_{t-1} - (1 - \alpha)cnd_{t-1} + \theta_1\pi_t + \theta_2\Delta\pi_t + v_t \tag{5.3}$$

where $|\alpha| < 1$ for stability

If further it is assumed that, in a steady state, with no inflation,

$$cnd_t = Ky_t^{\delta} \tag{5.4}$$

one obtains from equation (5.3) the long-run steady-state elasticity and the coefficient of proportionality as respectively

$$\delta = (\beta_1 + \beta_2) / (1 - \alpha) \text{ and } K = \exp[k + (\beta_1 - \delta)g / (1 - \alpha)] \tag{5.5}$$

where g is the steady state rate of growth of cnd and y. From (5.5) it follows that, imposing the restriction

$$\beta_1 + \beta_2 + \alpha = 1 \tag{5.6}$$

implies a long-run elasticity of unity ($\delta = 1$) and equation (5.3) reduces to

$$\Delta\log cnd_t = k + \beta_1\Delta\log y_t - (1 - \alpha)\log(cnd/y)_{t-1} + \theta_1\pi_t + \theta_2\Delta\pi_t + v_t \tag{5.7}$$

Equation (5.7) was the consumption function estimated by Davidson et al. (1978). It embodied the long run property of proportionality between consumers' expenditure and disposable income (equation (5.4)), in the presence of a unitary long run elasticity of consumption with respect to income (equation (5.6)). The fact that in a steady state, equation (5.4) was satisfied, reflected the requirement that the model, embodied by equation (5.7), be "theory consistent".

The reconciliation between the short dynamics of equation (5.7) and the steady state property of equation (5.4) was provided by an "error correction mechanism" (ECM), represented by the term $\Delta \log (cnd/y)_{t-1}$ in equation (5.7). [4]

Thus as long as cnd and y stayed on their steady state paths, ($cnd_{t-1} = Ky_{t-1}$), consumers would plan on spending each year the amount they spent the previous year ($cnd_t = cnd_{t-1}$) modified by a proportion of the annual change in income ($\beta_1 \Delta \log y_t$). If however in the previous period cnd and y departed from their steady state paths, there would, in the current period, be an attempt to adjust expenditure so as to correct this imbalance ($(1-\alpha) \log (cnd/y)_{t-1}$). Thus the ECM represented a feedback from the previous (cnd/y) ratio so as to ensure coherence between the short run consumption decision (equation (5.7)) and the long run target outcome (equation (5.4)). [5] Davidson et al. (1978) showed that their equation encompassed previous formulations of the UK consumption function by Hendry (1974), Ball et al. (1975) and Wall et al. (1975). Furthermore by estimating equation (5.7) over the period 1958 Q1 – 1970 Q4 (and retaining the 20 observations 1971 Q1 – 1975 Q5 purely for forecasting tests) they were able to show that their model was data coherent, in that it fitted the data well, both within the sample period and outside it.

Consumers' Expenditure and the Role of Liquid Assets, Hendry and Ungern-Sternberg (1981)

The Davidson et al. (1978) model was in turn encompassed by Hendry and Ungern-Sternberg (1981) who added an "integral correction term" to ensure stock as well as flow equilibrium. They argued that since inflation eroded real wealth, in the presence of a target ratio of wealth to income, agents needed to divert a part of their nominal incomes to restoring the real value of wealth. What was appropriate in studies of consumption was therefore a new measure of income, y^* obtained by deducting from personal disposable income y, the inflation induced losses on wealth. The consumption function was then defined in terms of this "inflation adjusted" income and also contained the stock of real wealth as an additional explanatory variable.

The difficulty of obtaining reliable measures of wealth was side-stepped by using instead the narrower concept of liquid assets. On this definition there were no capital gains to be made on wealth and the only capital losses would be purely inflation induced. In other words if all private wealth was liquid assets, then λ would take the value unity when y_t^* was defined as

$$y_t^* = y_t - \lambda \pi_t (M/p)_{t-1} \quad (5.8)$$

where M was the end period stock of liquid assets, L, net of bank advances and loans for house purchase.

However to the extent that liquid assets did not constitute all of wealth, the value of λ could not be assumed to be unity and had instead to be estimated. This was done by employing a grid search to minimise the residual sum of squares. The Hendry and Ungern-Sternberg (1981) consumption function was therefore represented by

$$\Delta \log cnd_t = \beta_0 + \beta_1 \Delta \log y_t^* + \beta_2 \log(cnd/y^*)_{t-1} + \beta_3 (L/py^*)_{t-1} + v_t \quad (5.9)$$

Two features of equation (5.9) deserve comment. First, criticism of the Deaton (1977) and the Davidson et al. (1978) models that inflation had an unbounded effect on the saving ratio, was no longer valid; instead the most one could now lose from inflation were ones liquid assets. Second, in addition to the ECM of Davidson et al. (1978), there was now a further control mechanism in the asset to income ratio. In other words in disequilibrium, an agent would adjust his consumption expenditure in an attempt to restore both flow equilibrium (in terms of a desired consumption/income ratio) and stock equilibrium (in terms of a desired asset/income ratio).

Hendry and Ungern-Sternberg (1981) estimated a quarterly version of equation (5.9) on UK data for the period 1962 Q4 – 1977 Q4 and obtained an estimate of λ (in equation (5.8)) of 0.5. Several interesting differences emerged between the estimates from this model and the earlier estimates from the Davidson et al. (1978) model which it encompassed. Firstly, the steady state assumption, $cnd = Ky$, of Davidson et al. (1978) seemed questionable in view of the strong and persistent seasonal behaviour of cnd/y. A steady state solution of the form $cnd = K_i y$, where K_i varied seasonally was more plausible. Second, the attempt by Davidson et al. (1978) to test for the significance of liquid assets by adding the variable L to equation (5.7) was inappropriate as it forced the steady state solution to be $cnd/y = Kf(L)$; it seemed more reasonable however to suppose $cnd/y = Kf(L/py)$. Finally Hendry and Ungern-Sternberg (1981) confirmed, like Deaton (1977) and Townend (1976), the importance of some cumulative measure in explaining aggregate real consumers' expenditure in the UK.

Consumers' Expenditure and the Role of Marketable Securities, Pesaran and Evans (1984)

A major drawback of the Hendry and Ungern-Sternberg (1981) model was that by considering only liquid assets, its definition of wealth was excessively narrow. As a consequence the stock flow relation in equation (5.9) which should have been represented by a total wealth/income ratio was (perhaps inadequately) proxied by a liquid assets/income ratio. A further consequence of this limited definition of personal wealth was of course that the influence on consumers' expenditure of capital gains and losses on marketable securities could not be considered. The major reason for the exclusion of non-liquid items from the definition of wealth was of course, as noted above, the absence of reliable data on these items. From this lacuna in the Hendry and Ungern-Sternberg (1981) model sprang the motivation for the Pesaran and Evans (1984) study of aggregate consumers' expenditure in the UK. Their purpose was to attempt a fuller treatment of wealth in the UK consumption function than had hitherto been adopted, by circumventing some of the data problems that bedevilled all researchers in this field. This they achieved through the econometric technique of "quasi-differencing" the data.

Pesaran and Evans started with a modified form of the Ando and Modigliani (1963) relationship, relating aggregate real consumption, c_t, to real disposable income, y_t, nominal initial assets, A_{t-1} and capital gains Z_{tj}, $(j = 1 \ldots m)$, [6] on a range of m assets with the last two variables deflated by the consumers' price index, p_t, to obtain

$$c_t = \alpha_0 + \alpha_1 y_t + \alpha_2 (A_{t-1}/p_t) + \sum_{j=1}^{m} \alpha_{3j} \frac{Z_{tj}}{p_t} + \eta_t$$

$$\alpha_0 \geq 0,\ \alpha_1 < 1,\ \alpha_2 > 0,\ \alpha_1 > \alpha_2,$$

$$0 \leq \alpha_{3j} \leq 1;\ t = 1 \ldots T \qquad (5.10)$$

where η_t is the disturbance term. In an unconstrained life cycle context equation (5.10) could be rationalised by assuming that expected real interest rates were fixed and that expected future incomes were proportional to current incomes; an alternative rationalisation is through the presence of liquidity constraints, whereby current income and assets provide a direct source of funds and also determine the possible size of borrowing.

However equation (5.10) as it stood could not be estimated since reliable measures of consumer asset holdings did not exist. A possible solution might have been to construct such a measure using the flow of saving to cumulate on an initial asset value, A_o, so that

$$A_t = A_0 + \sum_{i=1}^{t} p_i(y_i - c_i) + \sum_{i=1}^{t} G_i \tag{5.11}$$

where G_t was the nominal value of the aggregate capital gains or losses in period t. [7] Substituting equation (5.11) into (5.10) and transforming to solve for the real saving ratio, $s_t = 1 - c_t/y_t$, one obtained

$$s_t = (1 - \alpha_1) - (\alpha_0/y_t) - \alpha_2 A_0/Y_t - \alpha_2(\theta_t s_{t-1} + ... + \theta_2 s_1)$$
$$- \alpha_2 \sum_{i=1}^{t}(G_i/Y_t) - \sum_{j=1}^{m} \alpha_{3j}(Z_{tj}/Y_t) + v_t \tag{5.12}$$

where $Y_t = p_t y_t$ was income in current prices, $v_t = \eta_t/Y_t$ and $\theta_t = Y_{t-1}/Y_t$. The problem with estimating equation (5.12) – apart from the difficulty of obtaining reliable estimates of the initial stock A_o – was that if, because of measurement errors in y_t and c_t, there was a difference between the measured saving ratio $S_t = 1 - C_t/Y_t$, where C_t was consumption expenditure at current prices, and the true ratio, s_t, then the variance of the error term would rise over time. Thus if

$$S_t = s_t + w_t \tag{5.13}$$

then the substitution of (5.12) into (5.10) would result in the error term, $v_t + w_t + \alpha_2(\theta_t w_{t-1} + ... + \theta_2 w_1)$ where w_t is the measurement error. This in addition to having an increasing variance over time, would also be serially correlated and statistically dependent on the right-hand side variables. The solution to these problems was to substitute equation (5.13) into (5.12) and then to "quasi-difference", using θ_t, to obtain

$$S_t - \theta_t S_{t-1} = (1 - \alpha_1)(1 - \theta_t) - \alpha_0 \pi_t/\{(1 + \pi_t)y_t\}$$
$$- \alpha_2 \theta_t \{S_{t-1} + (G/Y)_{t-1}\}$$
$$- \sum_{j=1}^{m} \alpha_{3j}\{(Z_{tj}/Y_t) - \theta_t(Z_{t-1,j}/Y_{t-1})\} + u_t \tag{5.14}$$

where $u_t = v_t + w_t - \theta_t\{v_{t-1} + (1 - \alpha_2)w_{t-1}\}$

Equation (5.14) was then adopted by Pesaran and Evans (1984) as the equation to be estimated since (i) it did not involve the "unknown" term A_o, (ii) u_t had a simpler heteroscedastic structure than w_t and (iii) the autocorrelation of u_t, even if significant, would only be of the first-order. The Pesaran and Evans (1984) model encompassed other explanations of aggregate saving behaviour since equation (5.14) could be rewritten, ignoring the capital gains terms, as

$$S_t \cong (1 - \alpha_1)g_t + (1 - \alpha_1 - \alpha_0/y_t)\pi_t + (1 - \alpha_2)(1 - g_t - \pi_t)S_{t-1} \tag{5.15}$$

having replaced θ_t by $\{(1 + g_t)(1 + \pi_t)\}^{-1} \cong 1 - g_t - \pi_t$, where g_t was the rate of growth of real disposable income.

It is relatively straightforward to show that the Pesaran and Evans (1984) model encompasses the other three models discussed in this chapter. Equation (5.7) – the Davidson et al. (1978) equation – can be rewritten as

$$\Delta \log c_t = b_0 + b_1 \Delta \log y_t + b_2 \log (c/y)_{t-1} + b_3\pi_t + b_4\Delta\pi_t \tag{5.16}$$

which yields the approximation [8]

$$S_t \cong - b_0 + (1 - b_1)g_t - b_3\pi_t - b_4\Delta\pi_t + (1 + b_2)S_{t-1} \tag{5.17}$$

which apart from the term $\Delta\pi_t$, is also Deaton's (1977) equation. Comparing equations (5.15) and (5.17) with the equation (5.14) the Deaton (1977) and the Davidson et al. (1978) models will approximate the Pesaran and Evans (1984) model for small enough values of g_t and c_t.

Equation (5.14) also encompasses the Hendry and Ungern-Sternberg (1981) model since it has both a wider definition of wealth and also treats inflation induced losses separately rather than as a deduction from disposable income.

Pesaran and Evans estimated equation (5.14) on annual data for total consumers' expenditure over the period 1953-1981. Initially they considered capital gains terms on three assets: UK ordinary shares, British government securities, and a monetary asset comprising selected liquid assets less loans to the personal sector for house purchase. However, the coefficients on the latter two terms were found to be insignificantly different from zero and were dropped from the final equation. The empirical results, argued Pesaran and Evans (1984), showed that their model was consistent with the evidence. In particular capital gains and losses proved to be highly significant in explaining the saving ratio. Furthermore a comparative analysis of the model with those of Deaton (1977), Davidson et al. (1978) and Hendry and Ungern-Sternberg (1981) showed it to be superior in explaining total consumers' expenditure, both in terms of statistical fit and in terms of parsimony.

5.3 The UK Consumption Function Revisited

Against the background of the previous section's review of four major models of aggregate consumers' expenditure in the UK, this section turns to a revaluation of these models employing the concept of a household's "disposable resources" developed in Chapter 4. Tables 5.1-5.4 show the results of estimating the four models. Each of these tables presents, for the relevant model, three sets of estimates; for the periods 1955-86 and 1966-86 using the UKNA concepts of income and consumption and then for 1966-86 using concepts of household "disposable resources" and consumption developed in the preceding chapter. For each of the models, the estimates for the third equation (1966-86 household concept) are broadly similar to the estimates from the first two equations (1955-86 and 1966-86, UKNA personal sector concepts). [9] However several differences in the estimates, and inferences on the estimates, emerge when the income and consumption concepts are altered. One of the most important changes was that the coefficient on the inflation rate term in Deaton (1977) and the coefficient on the inflation rate and the change in the inflation rate terms in Davidson et al. (1978) were no longer significantly different from zero. Another change was that the coefficient on the lagged consumption to income ratio in the Davidson et al. (1978) model was, as in the 1966-86 UKNA version, not significantly different from zero though the coefficient on the same term in the Hendry and Ungern-Sternberg (1981) model was, like the other versions, significantly different from zero. Finally the estimate of λ, obtained through a maximum likelihood search, fell from 1.2 in the equations estimated on UKNA data to 0.55 in the equation estimated on household data.

It should be noted that the role of λ in the Hendry and Ungern-Sternberg (1981) model is to account for any scale effects due to wrongly choosing measures for π or (M/p); so that when $\lambda = 1$ consumers' perceive the entire inflation induced loss on net liquid assets as negative income. Thus the results presented imply that when the consumption function on

Table 5.1
Estimation Results for the Deaton (1977) Model

(Dependent variable: S_t)

Period	Constant	g_t	c_t	S_{t-1}	$\overline{R}^2$	$\hat{\sigma}$	u_t
1955-81	0.002	0.325	0.124	0.813	0.92	0.007	
(UKNA)	(0.47)	(5.30)	(4.15)	(14.79)	0.09	-0.39	AR2
1966-86	-0.002	0.296	0.156	0.828	0.84	0.007	
(UKNA)	(-0.19)	(4.25)	(4.07)	(7.15)			
1966-86	-0.009	0.434	0.109	0.849	0.84	0.012	
	(1.16)	(5.85)	(1.69)	(8.47)			

$\chi^2(1) = 1.64$ $\chi^2(1) = 0.14$; χ^2 statistics relate to the last equation only.
OLS AR1
AR1 AR2

Figures in parentheses represent t-values, $\hat{\sigma}$ is the equation standard error.

OLS, AR1, AR2 are respectively ordinary least squares and first and second order autoregressive processes respectively.

All the equations were estimated using Dr Hashem Pesaran's AR1 package.

Table 5.2
Estimation Results for the Davidson et al. (1978) Model
(Dependent Variable: $\Delta\log c_t$)

Period	Constant	$\Delta\log y_t$	$\log(c/y)_{t-1}$	π_t	$\Delta\pi_t$	$\overline{R}^2$	$\hat{\sigma}$	u_t
1955-86	-0.001	0.641	-0.180	-0.136	-0.014	0.84	0.008	
(UKNA)	(0.19)	(9.26)	(2.90)	(3.68)	(0.26)	0.05	-0.35	AR2
1966-86	0.013	0.706	-0.039	-0.119	-0.107	0.90	0.007	
(UKNA)	(1.86)	(13.93)	(-0.60)	(4.77)	(2.26)	-0.75	-0.45	AR2
1966-86	0.010	0.545	-0.152	-0.117	0.014	0.78	0.013	
	(1.14)	(6.67)	(1.44)	(1.58)	(0.16)			

$\chi^2(1) = 1.64$ $\chi^2(1) = 0.17$ log = natural logarithms
OLS AR1
AR1 AR2

Table 5.3
Estimation Results for the Hendry and Ungern-Sternberg (1981) Model

(Dependent variable: $\Delta \log c_t$)

Period	Constant	$\Delta\log y_t$	$\log(c/y^*)_{t-1}$	$\log(L/py^*)_{t-1}$	$\bar{R}^2$	$\hat{\sigma}$	u_t
1955-86	0.004	0.632	-0.414	0.081	0.81	0.009	
(UKNA)	(0.90)	(11.44)	(4.24)	(3.61)			
1966-86	0.004	0.769	-0.379	0.081	0.81	0.008	
(UKNA)	(1.32)	(18.68)	(6.77)	(7.62)	-0.888	-0.547	AR2
1966-86	0.006	0.547	-0.267	0.051	0.78	0.013	
	(1.10)	(8.16)	(2.02)	(1.54)			

$\chi^2(1) = 1.68$
OLS
AR1

$\chi^2(1) = 0.43$
AR1
AR2

L_t is the stock of personal sector holdings of liquid assets (end-period).

$y^*_t = y_t - \lambda\pi_t (M/p)_t$ (λ = 1.2, 1.2 and 0.55 respectively on a maximum likelihood search), where M_t is personal sector liquid asset holdings net of bank advances and loans for house purchase.

UKNA definitions was fitted to the personal sector this loss was overstated. In a similar vein, in the Pesaran and Evans (1984) model (Table 5.4), both capital gains on ordinary shares and on government securities exerted a significant influence on the personal sector saving ratio; however only gains on ordinary shares proved significant in explaining the household sector's saving ratio.

In order to obtain a common basis for comparison, the models were applied to total consumers' expenditure. However two of the models (Davidson et al. (1978) and Hendry and Ungern-Sternberg (1981)) and Ungern-Sternberg (1981)) were originally applied to non-durable consumers' expenditure only. Hence, to test for the effects of the definition changes, suggested in this and the previous chapter, on non-durable consumption, these two models were estimated, this time excluding expenditure on durable goods from the dependent variable. In doing so, the net availability of credit from the housing and credit markets was not excluded from "disposable resources" on the ground that, though such credit was primarily available for expenditure on durable goods, the availability of such credit, by releasing resources, could, nevertheless, have an indirect effect on non-durable consumption. The estimation results from such an exercise are shown in Tables 5.5 and 5.6. As will be apparent, the narrowing of focus does not alter the results in any significant manner. When the Davidson et al. (1978) model was applied to total consumption, the coefficient on the error correction term was only significantly different from zero over the period 1955-86. When the model was applied to non-durable consumption, this estimate continued to be significant over this period but not over the period 1966-86 (Table 5.5). Under the household definitions, with non-durable consumption as the dependent variable, the significance of the inflation term improved considerably in the Davidson et al. (1978) model. Finally in both models the coefficient estimate on $\Delta\log y_t$ dropped, as expected, quite considerably (Tables 5.5 and 5.6).

Table 5.4
Estimation Results for the Pesaran and Evans (1984) Model

(Dependent variables: $(S_t - \theta_t S_{t-1})$)

Period	$1-\theta_t$	$\pi_t/(1+\pi_t)y_{t-1}$	$S_{t-1}+(G/Y)_{t-1}$	DZS	DZB	$\bar{R}^2$	$\hat{\sigma}$	u_t
1955-86	0.379	-0.479	-0.023	-0.027	-0.186	0.40	0.111	
(UKNA)	(4.29)	(3.50)	(1.43)	(1.70)	(2.03)			
1966-86	0.244	-0.120	-0.078	-0.042	-0.448	0.69	0.067	
(UKNA)	(5.38)	(1.59)	(7.76)	(2.96)	(2.64)	-0.76	-0.51	AR2
1966-86	0.409	-0.441	-0.073	-0.040	-0.041	0.78	0.109	
	(6.26)	(5.09)	(3.11)	(2.74)	(0.21)	-0.45		AR1

$\chi^2(1) = 4.16$
OLS
AR1

$\chi^2(1) = 2.11$
AR1
AR2

All the variables have been deflated by $(1-\theta_t)$ to allow for heteroscedasticity.

$DZS = (Z_{ts}/y_t) - \theta_t(Z_{t-1},s/y_{t-1})$ $DZB = (Z_{tb}/y_t) - \theta_t(Z_{t-1,b}/Y_{t-1})$

where Z_{ts} and Z_{tb} are capital gains, net of general inflation, on ordinary shares and government securities.

Table 5.5
Estimation Results for the Davidson et al. (1978) Model

(Dependent variable: $\Delta\log cnd_t$)

Period	Constant	$\Delta\log y_t$	$\log(cnd/y)_{t-1}$	c_t	Δc_t	$\bar{R}^2$	$\hat{\sigma}$	u_t
1955-86	0.001	0.504	-0.104	-0.149	-0.020	0.89	0.005	
(UKNA)	(0.03)	(11.81)	(3.87)	(5.23)	(0.56)			
1966-86	0.003	0.522	-0.095	-0.158	-0.036	0.89	0.006	
(UKNA)	(0.26)	(9.48)	(1.84)	(4.52)	(0.83)			
1966-86	0.006	0.413	-0.072	-0.115	-0.072	0.73	0.011	
	(0.53)	(5.58)	(1.22)	(1.75)	(0.91)			

$\chi^2(1) = 0.54$
OLS
AR1

$\chi^2(1) = 0.25$
AR1
AR2

cnd is consumers' expenditure on non-durable goods and services at 1980 prices.

Table 5.6
Estimation Results for the Hendry and Ungern-Sternberg (1981) Model

(Dependent variable: $\Delta \log cnd_t$)

Period	Constant	$\Delta \log y_t$	$\log(cnd/y^*)_{t-1}$	$\log(L/py^*)_{t-1}$	$\bar{R}^2$	$\hat{\sigma}$	u_t
1955-86 (UKNA)	-0.006 (0.50)	0.496 (10.25)	-0.293 (3.73)	0.097 (3.92)	0.81	0.007	
1966-86 (UKNA)	-0.021 (2.15)	0.508 (9.26)	-0.392 (4.49)	0.109 (4.22)	0.83	0.009	
1966-86	-0.009 (0.85)	0.411 (6.51)	-0.166 (1.84)	0.054 (1.59)	0.69	0.012	

$\chi^2(1) = 0.19$
OLS
AR1

$\chi^2(1) = 0.39$
AR1
AR2

See also notes to Table 5.3.

5.4 The Cost of Borrowing and Consumer' Expenditure

An unsatisfactory feature of the "disposable resources" concept employed in this and the previous chapter, is the treatment of consumer credit as an exogenous flow. To allow for the possibility that consumers might choose the volume of such credit, conditional upon an exogenously given cost of borrowing, the equations were re-estimated, excluding net consumer credit from disposable resources, but, including in the equations, an additional term to reflect the cost of borrowing. These results are shown in Table 5.7.

Because of the presence of inflation effects, either direct or indirect, in the four models under review, the cost of consumer credit was taken to be the "real" cost, r_t, proxied in the empirical work by the difference between the Finance House Base Rate and the rate of change in the consumers' price deflator. All the four models except for Hendry and Ungern-Sternberg (1981) displayed significant and correctly signed interest rate effects, indicating that the earlier treatment of credit flows as exogenous, was mistaken. Under this revised treatment of consumer credit, many of the inferential changes, consequent upon adopting the new income and consumption definitions, disappeared. In particular, the inflation effects in the Deaton (1977) and Davidson et al. (1978) model continued to be significant.

It is interesting to note that the inclusion of the real rate of interest in the equations identifies two channels of influence of the inflation rate on consumers' expenditure. The first, *a la* Deaton (1977), means that a rise in the inflation rate has a negative effect on such expenditure. The second, indicates that, with given nominal rates of interest, a rise in the inflation rate, lowers the real cost of borrowing and hence has a positive effect on consumers' expenditure. The estimates indicate that the net effect of inflation on saving is positive.

Finally the equations (as specified in Table 5.7) were re-estimated to test whether the "net borrowing for house purchase" component of disposable resources had the same effect on consumption as the rest of disposable resources. The technique adopted to test this hypothesis followed closely the "liquid assets correction" of Hendry and Ungern-Sternberg (1981) and

Table 5.7
Estimation Results for the Four Consumption Models with the Cost of Borrowing Included as an Additional Variable

Deaton (1977):

$$S = \underset{(2.77)}{-0.033} + \underset{(5.54)}{0.435}\, g_t + \underset{(3.06)}{0.391}\, c_t + \underset{(2.34)}{0.288}\, r_t + \underset{(4.52)}{0.648}\, S_{t-1}$$

$\bar{R}^2 = 0.798$; $\chi^2(1) = 0.98$ (OLS, AR1); $\chi^2(1) = 0.03$ (AR1, AR2); $\hat{\sigma} = 0.112$

Davidson et al. (1978):

$$\Delta \log c_t = \underset{(2.57)}{0.034} + \underset{(6.44)}{0.548}\, \Delta \log y_t - \underset{(2.23)}{0.343}\, \log(c/y)_{t-1} - \underset{(2.73)}{0.396}\, \pi_t$$

$$- \underset{(0.23)}{0.020}\, \Delta\pi_t - \underset{(2.20)}{0.29}\, r_t$$

$\bar{R}^2 = 0.79$; $\chi^2(1) = 1.91$ (OLS, AR1); $\chi^2(1) = 1.21$ (AR1, AR2); $\hat{\sigma} = 0.012$

Hendry and Ungern-Sternberg (1981):

$$\Delta \log c_t = \underset{(1.13)}{0.006} + \underset{(6.65)}{0.597}\, \Delta \log y_t - \underset{(1.39)}{0.251}\, \log(c/y^*)_{t-1}$$

$$+ \underset{(1.12)}{0.040}\, \log(L/py^*)_{t-1} - \underset{(0.07)}{0.006}\, r_t$$

$\bar{R}^2 = 0.72$; $\chi^2(1) = 1.92$ (OLS, AR1); $\chi^2(1) = 0.37$ (AR1, AR2); $\hat{\sigma} = 0.014$

Pesaran and Evans (1984):

$$\underset{(5.05)}{0.363}\,(1-\theta_t) - \underset{(4.05)}{0.395}\,(\pi_t/(1+\pi_t)y_t) - \underset{(2.64)}{0.096}\,(S_{t-1} + (G/Y)_{t-1})$$

$$- \underset{(3.48)}{0.057}\, DZS - \underset{(1.02)}{0.214}\, DZB + \underset{(2.25)}{0.16}\, \hat{r}_t$$

$\bar{R}^2 = 0.82$; AR1 $= -0.50$; $\chi^2(1) = 5.29$ (OLS, AR1); $\chi^2(1) = 1.65$ (AR1, AR2); $\hat{\sigma} = 0.107$

The equations were estimated over 1966-86 using the household disposable resources and consumption definitions but with net consumer credit excluded from disposable resources.

r_t is the real rate of interest proxied by the Finance House Base Rate (Source: Financial Statistics) less the rate of change in the consumer price deflator (c_t); $\hat{r}_t = (r/Y)_t - \theta_t(r/Y)_{t-1}$) since in the Pesaran and Evans (1984) model, if r_t enters equation (5.10), $\hat{r}_t$ is the relevant variable for equation (5.14).

was as follows. Let h_t be the real value of net borrowing for house purchase [10] and let y_t^* be real disposable resources not including h_t. Then define total disposable resources as $y_t = y_t^* + \gamma h_t$. Under the definitions of this paper, γ has been implicitly set to unity so that the impact on consumption of y_t^* and h_t has been assumed to be the same. If however γ was greater (less) than unity, the marginal propensity to consume out of h_t, would be greater (less) than marginal propensity to consume out of y_t^*; in the extreme when $\gamma=0$, all of h_t would be saved. As with the determination of λ in the Hendry and Ungern-Sternberg (1981) model, the optimal value of γ was determined, for all the models, by a maximum likelihood search. The maximum likelihood values of γ obtained were $\gamma^*=1.6$, 0.6 and 0.5 for the Deaton (1977), Davidson et al. (1978) and Ungern-Sternberg (1981) models, with the implication that the propensity to consume out of net resources from the housing market was less than the propensity to consume out of the remainder of disposable resources. However a likelihood ratio test did not reject the null hypothesis, $\gamma=1$ against the alternative, $\gamma=\gamma^*$. For the Pesaran and Evans (1984) model the likelihood function was extremely flat and experimenting with different values of γ produced little change in the likelihood value. Since for none of the models were the parameter estimates with $\gamma=\gamma^*$ very different from the estimates with $\gamma=1$, the former set of estimates are not reproduced.

5.5 The Influence of Committed Saving on Discretionary Saving

One of the consequences of adopting the approach to analysing household behaviour outlined in the preceding chapter, is that a distinction emerges between discretionary and committed saving The consumption/saving function estimates presented in the third row of Tables 5.1-5.4 relate only to discretionary saving, the volume of committed saving being determined by previous contracts. The purpose of this section is to test whether committed saving have any influence on the discretionary saving decision, where, as noted in chapter 4, in any period t, committed saving are regarded as being composed of (i) the net surplus of life assurance companies and pension funds, LAS and (ii) regular payments of mortgage principal, MGR. [11]

In order to answer this question, it was assumed that, in addition to the influences represented in equation (5.10) aggregate consumption was also influenced by the real value of pension fund wealth, (W_t/p_t), [12] and by the real value of the stock of housing equity, (H_t/p_t), so that equation (5.10) now acquired an additional term, $\alpha\{(W_t/p_t)+(H_t/p_t)\}$, $\alpha \geq 0$.

If the current values of W and H were obtained by cumulating on an initial value, then

$$W_t = W_0 + \sum_{i=1}^{t} LAS_i \qquad (5.18)$$

$$H_t = H_0 + \sum_{i=1}^{t} MGR_i \qquad (5.19)$$

Quasi-differencing using θ_t now meant that equation (5.14), which was the original equation estimated, would now contain an additional term, $z_t=\theta_t(W_t+H_t)/Y_{t-1}$. Estimating equation (5.14) with this additional term, yielded the following regression:

$$\begin{aligned} s_t - \theta_t s_{t-1} = {} & \underset{(6.25)}{0.401}\,(1-\theta_t) - \underset{(5.09)}{0.417}\,(c_t/(1+c_t)y_t) \\ & - \underset{(2.60)}{0.136}\,(s_{t-1} + (G/Y)_{t-1}) - \underset{(2.83)}{0.052}\,DZS - \underset{(1.04)}{0.241}\,DZB + \underset{(2.01)}{0.362}\,\hat{r}_t - \underset{(0.37)}{0.029}\,z_t \end{aligned}$$

$\bar{R}^2 = 0.68$ AR1 = 0.60; $\chi^2_{OLS/AR1}(1) = 7.64$; $\chi^2_{AR1/AR2}(1) = 3.78$; $\hat{\sigma} = 0.103$

Thus on the basis of the above regression there did not appear to be any evidence that committed saving exercised a significant influence on the discretionary saving ratio. This conclusion remained unchanged when the committed saving terms were tried separately, though , it must be admitted, that owing to the small sample size this conclusion, must necessarily be tentative.

5.6 Concluding Remarks

In the light of the detailed set of household accounts constructed in the previous chapter, four recent models of consumption/saving behaviour in the UK were reappraised in this chapter. From this reappraisal, three main results emerged. Firstly, the Pesaran and Evans (1984) model, which encompassed the earlier studies cited, was the most robust under these revisions. Secondly, the revisions indicated that explanations of aggregate saving or aggregate consumers' expenditure which ignored the real cost of borrowing on hire-purchase were perhaps misspecified. With such a variable included a second channel for the influence of inflation on saving could be identified. Finally although the revisions resulted in a distinction between discretionary and committed saving, there was little evidence that the discrctionary saving of households was affected by their committed saving.

NOTES

[1] Deaton (1977) and Pesaran and Evans (1984) estimated their models on quarterly and annual data respectively employing as their dependent variable, the aggregate saving ratio derived from total consumers' expenditure. Davidson et al. (1978) and Hendry and Ungern-Sternberg (1981) used quarterly, unadjusted data to explain movements in the total of consumers' expenditure on non-durable goods and services.

[2] See Townend (1976) and Deaton (1983) for a review of some of this literature.

[3] See Hendry (1983) for a detailed discussion of these aspects of econometric modelling.

[4] See Salmon (1982) for a detailed exposition on ECMs.

[5] Davidson and Hendry (1981) have shown that the ECM model, represented by equation (5.7), encompasses the permanent income-rational expectations model of Hall (1978).

[6] Z_{tj} is the gain or loss on the jth asset induced by changes in its price, net of changes in consumer prices, and defined as $Z_{tj}=(\pi_{tj}-\pi_t)A_{t-1}$, where π_{tj} and π_t are respectively $\Delta \log p_{tj}$ and $\Delta \log p_t$, p_{tj} being the price in period t, of the jth asset.

[7] Defined as $\Sigma\pi_{tj} A_{t-1\,j}$

[8] By first rewriting the dependent variable as $\log(c/y)_t$ and then noting that $\log(c/y)_t=\log(1-S_t)\cong -S_t$

[9] The detailed interpretation of the coefficients are to be found in the original papers and are not discussed here.

[10] The nominal value of net borrowing deflated by the consumers' price index.

[11] The model used to test this is that of Pesaran and Evans (1984) which encompasses the other models.

[12] Both W and H enter the consumption contemporaneously since it is assumed that decisions relating to them are prior to the consumption decision.

6. The distribution of income and aggregated consumers' expenditure

6.1 Introduction

The relationship between the aggregate of consumers' expenditure and disposable income is one of the most thoroughly researched areas in UK economics. [1] Although these studies have employed different methodologies to estimate consumption functions over different time periods, they have in common the fact that they all ignore the role of income distribution in influencing the aggregate volume of consumption. [2] (Notable exceptions to this general statement are studies by Doorn (1975) and Simmons (1980)). Since in Keynes' own analysis (cf. Keynes (1936), ch. 24) both the level of income and the manner of its distribution were seen as important determinants of aggregate consumption, this untested assumption of independence between aggregate consumption and income distribution may perhaps appear surprising.

Blinder (1975) explained this omission by arguing that "with the ascendancy of the Friedman (1957) and Modigliani and Brumberg (1954) models of consumer behaviour" the view that income distribution affected aggregate consumption "fell into disrepute in academic circles. It was supplanted by the view that marginal, and perhaps even average, propensities to consume are constant over the income distribution" (pp.447-8). The life-cycle model, as is well known, derives the aggregate consumption function from the hypothesis that the consumer chooses the time path of consumption which maximises lifetime utility, subject to the constraint that the present discounted value of all consumption, plus the present discounted value of the bequest (if any), is equal to lifetime disposable resources. A consequence of such a hypothesis is that consumption at each instant is proportional to lifetime disposable resources, with the constant of proportionality dependent only on age, length of life, the rate of interest and tastes.

However Blinder (1975) went on to show that even under the "life cycle" hypothesis, provided that the marginal utility of bequests, say β, was different from the marginal utility of income, say α, the redistribution of income among individuals who were alike in every respect, save permanent income, would alter aggregate consumption. In other words the independence of aggregate consumption and income distribution followed from the life cycle model only if it was assumed that either there were no bequests or that, if there were bequests, then $\alpha = \beta$. In attempting to test the influence of income distribution on aggregate consumption, Blinder (1975), constrained by lack of data, adopted what he termed "several second-best procedures". One of these consisted of estimating an aggregate consumption function (ie. aggregated over expenditure and over all households) by including in the function some conventional measure of inequality. This was also the approach adopted by Doorn (1975), who estimated log-linear expenditure functions, with the variance of the logarithms included as an explanatory variable, for 11 regions in the UK and for five main expenditure groups. A general conclusion of both studies was that the role of income distribution in influencing expenditure decisions was, at best, quite weak.

In this context, this chapter explores this topic further, by pursuing a suggestion by Blinder (1975), namely that "the only rigorously correct way to test for the existence of distribution effects in the aggregate consumption function is to estimate directly separate marginal propensities to consume by income class" (p.471). The aim of this chapter is to attempt to provide such a test for the United Kingdom. This was done by using data from the Family Expenditure Survey (FES) to construct, over the period 1963-86, annual data on income and consumption by quintiles. Separate consumption functions were then estimated for each quintile, using the "error correction" technique of Davidson et al. (1978), and the results were then used to test whether there were, or there were not, significant differences in the consumption behaviour of households in different quintiles. [3] The existence of such differences would of course suggest that consumption functions which treated all households as a single behavioural unit might be misleading, in so far as they ignored the differential behaviour of the constituent micro units.

There does not exist in the literature an unanimous view on the appropriate measure of consumers' expenditure to use in studying the consumption function. [4] This chapter employs total consumer's expenditure as the operational concept. This is line with the approach adopted in the previous chapter and has the advantage that it is directly translatable in terms of the economy's saving ratio. In estimating quintile specific consumption functions, the quintile estimates are compared to the "aggregate" estimates obtained both by aggregating over all the households in the FES and also by employing the UK national accounts (UKNA) data for the personal sector.

The organisation of the chapter is as follows: sections 2 and 3 describe, respectively, changes in the distribution of income that have occurred in the United Kingdom over the sample period 1963-86 and movements in the saving ratio of the different quintiles; section 4 presents the econometric results and the results of a simulation exercise are shown in section 5, with section 6 concluding the chapter.

6.2 Changes in the Distribution of Income in the UK, 1963-86

The income and expenditure data used in this paper are taken from the published annual reports of the FES for the years 1963-86. The FES is the only regular source of data containing information on consumption behaviour by income group. Average household expenditure on goods and services is presented in these reports for households grouped into bands on the basis of "gross" income. [5] The FES presentation of household expenditure by gross income bands includes, in addition to a detailed classification of expenditure on commodities and services, a supplementary listing of "other payments recorded". Among these other payments are income tax payments and national insurance contributions (by employees and the self-employed). For each income band the average tax and contribution payments were deducted from average gross income to arrive at the concept of disposable income used in this analysis of saving behaviour. Differences between the FES household data and the personal sector data of the UKNA have been discussed in Chapter 4 and will not be detailed here; nor will the deficiencies in the FES data, which are well documented in

Atkinson and Micklewright (1983).

Using these data, time series for income and expenditure by quintile (denoted Q1 (lowest) to Q5 (highest)) were constructed for the period 1963-86 using linear interpolation on the standard published tables based on nominal income bands. That is, to say, the nominal income bands were amalgamated (and split where necessary) to give, for each year, five bands ranked in ascending order of gross income, with 20 per cent of the total number of households in the sample allocated to each band. Errors in this procedure would arise when the published income bands straddled quintile endpoints. Of the income which accrued in aggregate to the households belonging to such a straddling band, the proportion allocated to the lower of the two quintiles was set equal to the fraction of the number of households in the band which was required to bring the cumulative proportion of households in the sample up to the multiple of 20 per cent which defined the endpoint between the two quintiles in question. The same proportion, calculated in this way to allocate gross income, was also used to allocate consumers' expenditure, tax payments, national insurance contributions and social security benefits of the straddling band. The disposable income of each quintile was calculated as the total gross income allocated to the quintile minus the total tax payments and national insurance contributions allocated to it. Similarly the "original" income of each quintile was calculated by subtracting total social security benefits allocated to the quintile from its allocated gross income. The CSO employs this concept of "original" income in its assessments of the net redistributive impacts of the tax/transfer system.

It is interesting to note, by way of digression, that Blinder's (1975) conclusion that, for the United States, distributive shares are not an adequate proxy for the size distribution of income also appears to be true for the United Kingdom. With regard to labour and transfer income, Table 6.1 shows that if the lowest (Q1) and the highest (Q5) quintiles are compared, there is a clear and strong association between income source and the size distribution of income. In the middle quintiles the association is still present but markedly less pronounced. With regard to the other forms of income, much weaker associations are observed and indeed income received in the form of private pensions and annuities comes near to being uniformly distributed between the quintiles Q2 to Q5. Even for social-security benefits it appears that households in the upper 40 per cent of the income distribution receive more than 20 per cent of income distributed in this form. Thus, knowing the form in which a pound is received does not unambiguously locate the recipient household in the distribution of income by size.

An indication of how the distribution of households income has changed over time in the UK is provided by Figure 6.1 and by Tables 6.2 and 6.3. Figure 6.1 plots the values of the Gini coefficients [6] for both original and disposable income for the period 1963-86, while Tables 6.2 and 6.3 present, for the period 1976-86, quintile shares in total original and disposable income respectively. It is apparent from Figure 6.1 that movements in income distribution displayed marked differences between the two sub-periods 1963-78 and 1979-86. Over the period 1963-78 there was a considerable increase in the degree of inequality associated with the distribution of original income, with its Gini coefficient rising from 0.28 in 1965 to 0.41 in 1978. Over the same period however the operation of the tax and transfer system ensured that the degree of inequality associated with the distribution of disposable income remained virtually unchanged, with its Gini coefficient remaining steady at around 0.29. To put the matter differently, in 1965 the shares of Q1 and Q5 in total original income were respectively 3.3 and 40.7 per cent; by 1978 their respective shares were 1.7 and 43.4 per cent. By way of contrast, the share of Q1 in total disposable income fell only slightly from 7.2 per cent in 1965 to 6.9 per cent in 1978, while the share of Q5 in total disposable income was greater, in 1978, by only 1 percentage point over its 1965 value of 36.7 per cent. Thus, upto Mrs Thatcher's first Tory government, public policy was a major instrument in preventing the growth of income inequalities in the UK. [7]

The period 1979-86 tells a different story. Here the rise in inequality in the distribution of original income – exemplified by its Gini coefficient rising from 0.42 in 1979 to 0.47 in 1986 – was met with only a feeble attempt at preventing this rise through the operation of the system of taxes and transfers. As a consequence the degree of inequality associated with the

Table 6.1
Joint Distribution of Gross Income, by Source and by Quintile, 1986

Quint-iles	% across / % down	Wages and Salaries	Self Employment	Imputed Housing	Invest-ment	Private Pension & Income	Other Sources	Social Security	All Sources
		SOURCE							
Q1	% across	3.9	1.2	5.5	3.0	4.6	1.9	79.9	100
	% down	0.2	0.0	4.8	3.3	4.8	8.0	28.3	4.6
Q2	% across	28.2	5.2	7.3	4.7	8.6	2.2	43.7	100
	% down	4.2	7.2	12.9	10.8	18.8	19.0	32.2	9.5
Q3	% across	60.3	6.9	6.0	4.6	6.9	1.1	14.1	100
	% down	15.6	14.9	18.5	18.3	26.2	16.5	18.0	16.6
Q4	% across	74.0	6.0	5.6	3.3	4.0	0.8	6.2	100
	% down	28.7	19.5	25.9	19.7	22.8	20.3	11.9	24.9
Q5	% across	74.4	10.1	4.6	4.5	2.7	0.9	2.8	100
	% down	51.3	58.4	37.9	47.9	27.4	36.2	9.6	44.4
All Households	% across	64.3	7.7	5.4	4.2	4.3	1.1	13.0	100
	% down	100	100	100	100	100	100	100	100

Source: FES 1986, Table 22, p. 66.

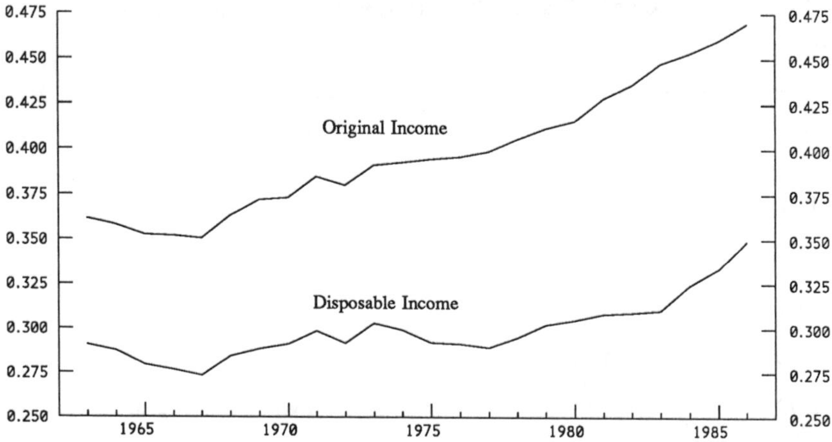

Figure 6.1 Distribution of Nominal Income by Households: Gini Coefficents for 1963-86

Source: Own calculations from FES data

distribution of disposable income also rose over this period, with the Gini coefficient on disposable income going up from 0.30 in 1979 to 0.35 in 1986. The deterioration in the share of disposable income of the poorest 40 per cent of households (with a corresponding improvement in the position of the top 20 per cent of households) can be seen from Table 6.3. In 1966 households in Q1 received 7.21 per cent of disposable income. Over the next 10 years this share dropped slightly reaching 7.02 per cent by 1976. Over the next 10 years this share fell sharply to its 1986 value of 5.54 per cent. As will be evident from the Table most of this deterioration took place in the years since 1979.

6.3 Saving By Income Class

The above discussion on the distribution of income has a direct bearing on an important target of macroeconomic policy, namely the aggregate household saving ratio. [8] The saving ratio of the household sector is a weighted average of the saving ratios of the households belonging to the different income classes, the weights being the proportions of the household sector's total disposable income that accrues to each income class. Changes in the aggregate saving ratio are thus brought about either through changes in the saving ratio of one or more of the income classes, or through the allocation of disposable income between the income classes. In this section we examine the influence of these two factors, relating respectively to differential saving behaviour and to differential income shares, on the household sector's saving ratio. In order to do so, the saving ratios for households in the five quintiles Q1-Q5, as well as for the aggregate of households, were first calculated and then plotted in Figure 6.2 for the period 1963-86. The differences between households in the different quintiles, with regard to the fraction of their disposable incomes saved, is immediately obvious from Figure 6.2. At no time over the period did households in either Q1 or Q2 have a positive saving ratio. The saving ratio for households in Q3 averaged about 0.5 per cent for the period. The fact that the UK household sector, in aggregate, saved on average 5 per cent of its disposable income was due firstly to the low weights attached to the negative saving of the poorest 40 per cent of households and secondly to the high weights attached to the positive saving of the top 40 per cent of households. Collectively, the former type of households received, over

Table 6.2
Quintile Shares in Total Original Income, 1966 and 1976-86

	Q1	Q2	Q3	Q4	Q5
1966	3.22	12.52	18.44	24.72	41.11
1976	2.09	9.80	18.52	26.26	43.33
1977	1.47	9.89	18.87	27.01	42.76
1978	1.68	9.23	18.73	26.74	43.61
1979	1.40	9.02	18.89	26.70	43.98
1980	1.44	8.84	18.46	26.92	44.34
1981	1.46	8.23	17.87	26.70	45.74
1982	1.42	7.43	18.07	26.99	46.09
1983	1.41	6.86	17.56	26.83	47.34
1984	1.17	6.82	17.20	27.23	47.58
1985	1.03	6.52	16.90	27.50	48.06
1986	1.08	6.18	16.42	26.95	49.37

Source: own calculations from FES data

1963-86, on average, less than 20 per cent of disposable income in the UK.

It is impossible for a fixed group of households to continually spend more than it currently receives. The consistently negative saving ratios of households in the two lowest income quintiles are only sustainable because the households comprising these quintiles are not fixed. Three different types of household are to be found in the lowest quintile. One type consists of the "permanently" poor households – households who start life with few or lowly rewarded natural endowments and who never receive, throughout their lifetime, transfer payments sufficient to lift them above the bottom of the income distribution. It is unlikely that the saving ratio for "permanently" poor households is much different from zero.

The other two main types of household in the lowest quintile are the "contingently" poor – they are there for only part of their lifetime. There are two such types, corresponding to the two ends of the life-cycle. At the "young" end there are households able to spend more than their current receipts because they can borrow against their future earnings. Relatively, however, it is households at the "older" end of the life cycle who dominate the lowest quintile. These are retired households, able to spend more than current receipts by dissaving from wealth accumulated during the years that they were economically active. The FES demonstrates the preponderance of elderly households in the lowest quintile. Households in this quintile are relatively small, contain disproportionately few children and working adults,

Table 6.3

Quintile Shares in Total Disposable Income, 1966 and 1976-86

	Q1	Q2	Q3	Q4	Q5
1966	7.21	13.74	18.50	23.76	36.79
1976	7.02	12.77	18.33	24.15	37.73
1977	6.88	12.80	18.54	24.67	37.10
1978	6.90	12.43	18.39	24.59	37.69
1979	6.56	12.19	18.55	24.55	38.15
1980	6.43	12.25	18.33	24.70	38.29
1981	6.73	11.99	17.87	24.35	39.06
1982	6.77	11.87	17.83	24.41	39.11
1983	6.82	11.88	17.69	24.17	39.44
1984	5.99	11.59	17.76	24.69	39.97
1985	5.76	11.28	17.43	24.85	40.68
1986	5.54	10.71	17.01	24.45	42.29

Source: own calculations from FES data

and a relatively large number of retired persons. The average age of the household head, is generally above the pension age for women and close to the male pension age.

Apart from inter-quintile differences in the level of the saving ratio, differences in the movements of this ratio between quintiles are also worthy of note. It is evident, for example, from Figure 6.2 that households in the upper quintiles Q3, Q4 and Q5 contributed little to the upward trend in saving over 1972-78. The most dramatic rise in saving (or more precisely, fall in dissaving) over this period was manifested by households in the lowest two quintiles. The size of this change was sufficiently great to have been a major contributor to the rise in the aggregate saving ratio over 1972-78, despite the low weight attached to these households in the formation of the aggregate saving ratio.

Over the earlier period, 1967-72, the aggregate saving ratio was approximately constant. A theory of aggregate saving behaviour, based on the notion of a single representative household, would have to appeal to counterbalancing influences on this single household in order to explain the observed near-constancy. In fact from Figure 6.2 it is evident that few households experienced such counterbalancing influences on their behaviour. The aggregate effect was due to reduced saving on the part of low-income households in Q1 and Q2 being offset by increased saving by high income households in Q5. Even if it is assumed that the same factors relating to the economic environment (for example, inflation rates, interest rates)

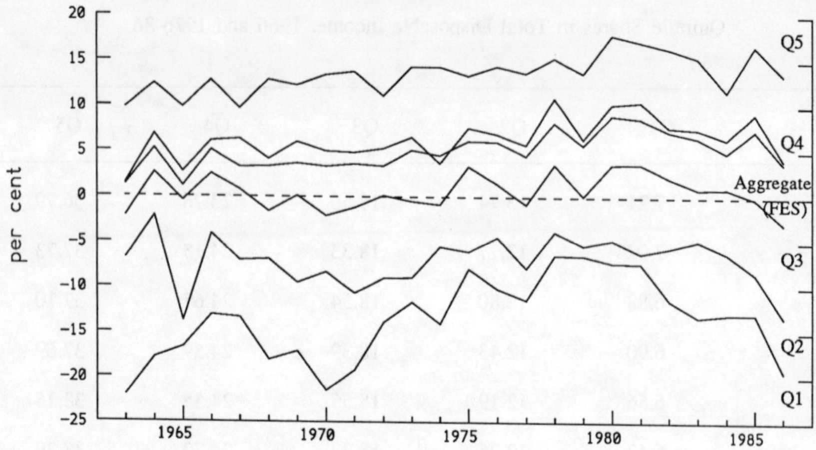

Figure 6.2 Saving Ratio by Quintiles, 1963-86

Source: FES Annual Reports

were operating equally on all the households, then it would appear that a household's behavioural response to these factors depended significantly on its position in the income distribution.

However different sets of economic factors affect different household types differently. It would therefore appear to be necessary to disaggregate households by income in order to isolate distinct groups of households and the specific sets of factors which determine their behaviour. It is often argued, in this connection, that households at the lower end of the income distribution are effectively excluded from participation, as borrowers, in capital markets and thus, for them, variations in the availability or cost of credit are of no concern. Changes in the expected uprating of social security benefits, on the other hand, may be of major concern to such households but of little concern to those at the upper end of the distribution. The next section attempts an econometric analysis of the responses of consumption expenditure to variations in the disposable income of households in the different quintiles.

6.4 Estimation and Inference

In this section the estimation and inference results for the aggregate consumption function, for each of the income quintiles, are presented. The previous chapter discussed four major studies of the UK consumption function undertaken over the past decade and noted that each study represented a contribution to applied econometric methodology. The first of these studies, that of Deaton (1977), looked at the effect of unanticipated inflation on involuntary saving. The second of these studies, that of Davidson et al. (1978), employed an "error-correction" mechanism (ECM) to provide a reconciliation between the long run equilibrium and the short run dynamics; this was followed by Hendry and Ungern-Sternberg (1981) who in addition to the ECM of Davidson et al (1978), also employed liquid assets as an "integral control" mechanism; the fourth model was that of Pesaran and Evans (1984) who employed a wider definition of wealth via the technique of "quasi-differencing". [9] The estimation of the last two models is however only possible in the presence of time series data on asset holdings. Since such data is not available by income class, this paper models the aggregate

Since such data is not available by income class, this paper models the aggregate consumption-income relationship, for each quintile, employing the methodology of Davidson et al (1978). Although the details of this methodology have been set out in the previous chapter, for ease of reference it is reproduced below.

The starting point is a general dynamic relation between real consumption, c_t, and real income, y_t, with inflation effects included so that

$$\alpha(L)\log c_t = k + \beta(L)\log y_t + \theta_1 c_t + \theta_2 \Delta\pi_t + v_t \qquad (t=1, ...,T), \qquad (6.1)$$

where t is a time subscript; π is the inflation rate, defined as the rate of change in the consumers' price deflator; Δ is the first difference operator; $\alpha(L)$ and $\beta(L)$ are polynomials in the lag operator, L; k is the intercept, and v is an error term.

If it is assumed that $\alpha(L)$ and $\beta(L)$ are of the first order, one obtains:

$$\Delta\log c_t = k + \beta_1 \Delta\log y_t + (\beta_1 + \beta_2)\log y_{t-1} - (1-\alpha)\log c_{t-1} + \theta_1 \pi_t + \theta_2 \Delta\pi_t + v_t \qquad (6.2)$$

where $|\alpha|<1$ for stability.

If further it is assumed that, in a steady state, with no inflation,

$$c_t = Ky^{\delta}_t \qquad (6.3)$$

one obtains from equation (6.2) the long-run steady-state elasticity and the coefficient of proportionality as respectively

$$\delta = (\beta_1 + \beta_2)/(1-\alpha) \text{ and } K = \exp[k + (\beta_1 - \delta)g/(1-\alpha)] \qquad (6.4)$$

where g is the steady state rate of growth of c and y. From (6.4) it follows that, imposing the restriction

$$\beta_1 + \beta_2 + \alpha = 1 \qquad (6.5)$$

implies a long-run elasticity of unity ($\delta=1$) and equation (6.2) reduces to

$$\Delta\log c_t = k + \beta_1 \Delta\log y_t - (1-\alpha)\log (c/y)_{t-1} + \theta_1\pi_t + \theta_2 \Delta\pi_t + v_t \qquad (6.6)$$

As Davidson et al (1978) point out, a feature of equation (6.6) is that if the observations on c and y lie close to their steady state path, so that, over the sample, equation (6.3) was approximately true, then the "error correction term" $\log (c/y)_{t-1}$ and the intercept k would be almost perfectly collinear. Although either regressor could, as a consequence, be dropped without much loss to the goodness-of-fit, setting $k=0$ would not affect long-run behaviour, but setting $1-\alpha=0$ would. [10] Accordingly, equation (6.6) was estimated, both with and without an intercept term on data for each quintile and on data obtained by aggregating over the quintiles, and the final choice of estimates was determined by whether the presence of the intercept adversely affected the significance level of the coefficient estimate on the error correction term. These results are shown in Table 6.4 and the implied long run properties of the estimated equations are summarized in Table 6.5.

The penultimate line of Table 6.4 refers to results obtained from aggregating the data over the quintiles and the last line of the same table refers to the corresponding results obtained using UKNA data for the personal sector and UKNA definitions of personal consumers' expenditure and disposable income. Since consumption functions for the UK have typically been estimated on UKNA data, this allows for comparability between existing estimates and the estimates of this chapter.

The estimation strategy was to first estimate equations (6.2) and (6.6) and to employ a likelihood ratio test for the null hypothesis: $\beta_1+\beta_2+\alpha=1$. In all cases the test indicated that this restriction was not rejected by the data at the 5 per cent level of significance. Given the specification of equation (6.6) the next test was to introduce an income inequality term explicitly as an explanatory variable in the aggregate (FES) and aggregate (UKNA) equations to see whether one could thereby obtain a parsimonious representation of the effects of income distribution on consumption. This inequality term was introduced as $\Delta \log G_t$, where G was the Gini coefficient on the distribution of disposable income by quintiles, shown in Figure 6.1. [11] For neither equation was the coefficient on $\Delta \log G_t$ significantly different from zero. A reasonable conclusion was thus that the effects of income distribution (if any) on consumption were being inadequately captured by the inclusion of an income inequality term in the aggregate equations. It should be noted, in passing, that these experiments were very similar to the ones conducted by Blinder (1975) and over which he expressed considerable dissatisfaction.

To test for the possibility that changes in a household's real consumption was, in addition to the variables already considered, also influenced by changes in the size of the household, equation (6.6) was re-estimated, for each quintile, with the variable $\Delta \log z_t$, included as an additional explanatory variable where z_t, was the average size of household in the quintile. [12] The coefficient on this variable, however, failed to be significantly different from zero. This was perhaps not surprising because, although over the sample period there was some evidence of a secular decline in the size of households for all quintiles, this decline was very gradual and year-on-year changes were almost imperceptible.

Following this, the next test was to see whether the propensity to consume out of incomes from public authority grants was different from the propensity to consume out of income from other sources. Thus, for example, Townend (1976) felt it was "reasonable to expect income from current grants from public authorities to be consumed more rapidly than income from other sources" (p.60) and he consequently imposed a long-run propensity to consume of unity on such income, leaving the propensity to consume out of non-grant income to be freely determined. To test for the possibly different propensities to consume out of grants income, equation (6.6) was re-estimated with an additional term $\Delta(y^g/y)_t$, where y^g was the real value of public authority grants. [13] This re-estimation was carried out for all the quintiles and for the aggregate (FES) and aggregate (UKNA) equations. For none of the equations, however, was the coefficient on $\Delta(y^g/y)_t$ significantly different from zero, thus implying that the null hypothesis that the propensity to consume out of grant and non-grant income was the same, could not be rejected by the data.

Table 6.4 provides prima facie evidence that there exist differences in the consumption behaviour of the different quintiles; this was formally tested for by estimating the quintile equations as a system using Zellner's (1962) seemingly unrelated regression equations (SURE) technique. Thus if β_i is the vector of slope coefficients of the equations (as specified in Table 6.4) for the ith quintile (i=1...5), the null hypothesis of no aggregation bias, $H_0:\beta_1=\beta_2...=\beta_5$ was not accepted by the data, at the 5 per cent level of level of significance, with a F(16,80) value of 2.72. After this, the possible equality of the individual coefficients across the quintiles was tested. Thus if β_{ij} is the jth slope coefficient in the equation for the ith quintile the four hypotheses that were tested were

$$H_{0j}: \beta_{1j} = \beta_{2j} ... = \beta_{5j} \ (j = 1...4).$$

This hypothesis was not accepted by the data for the coefficients on $\Delta \log y_t$ and $\log(c/y)_{t-1}$ with F(4, 90) values of 2.54 and 3.89. For the coefficients on π and $\Delta\pi$ however, this hypothesis was not rejected with F(4, 90) values of 1.44 and 1.67. Hence, it would appear that the quintiles differed from each other in terms of their consumption responses to changes in the disposable incomes. Their consumption responses to the inflation rate, and to changes in the inflation rate, did not however appear to be significantly different.

Table 6.4
Estimation Results of Equation (6.6), 1963-86

(Dependent variable: $\Delta \log c_t$)

Quintile	Intercept	$\Delta \log y_t$	$\log(c/y)_{t-1}$	c_t	Δct	$\chi^2(1)$	$\chi^2(1)$	$\chi^2(2)$	$\chi^2(4)$	$\bar{R}^2$	s
1	0.093	0.931	-0.511	-0.378	0.219	0.02	4.53	1.23	5.66	0.690	0.026
	(2.75)	(6.51)	(2.64)	(2.20)	(0.90)						
2	0.061	0.983	-0.582	-0.243	0.311	2.13	0.06	1.40	8.30	0.725	0.017
	(2.91)	(6.77)	(2.28)	(3.20)	(1.83)						
3	0.017	0.903	-0.935	-0.261	0.299	0.73	0.07	0.97	3.61	0.716	0.017
	(1.72)	(5.69)	(3.63)	(2.75)	(2.08)						
4	-0.037	0.778	-0.959	-0.294	0.476	0.00	1.98	0.97	5.18	0.677	0.020
	(1.96)	(4.15)	(4.60)	(2.54)	(2.88)						
5	-0.081	0.687	-0.768	-0.334	0.140	1.64	4.15	0.82	10.12	0.734	0.020
	(2.81)	(5.66)	(3.92)	(2.83)	(0.824)						
Aggregate	-0.010	0.707	-0.656	-0.299	0.242	0.72	2.70	0.55	8.58	0.682	0.016
(FES)	(0.46)	(5.12)	(3.37)	(3.24)	(1.78)						
Aggregate	-0.013	0.709	-0.279	-0.157	0.053	1.98	0.34	1.23	5.24	0.786	0.010
(UKNA)	(0.70)	(7.49)	(1.62)	(2.22)	(0.62)						

Figures in parantheses are t-values; s is the equation standard error.

The diagnostic tests based on the X^2 distribution are respectively: the Lagrange multiplier test for serial correlation (cf. Godfrey (1978)); Ramsey's (1969) RESET test for functional form misspecification; the Bera and Jarque (1981) test for normality of residuals and Chow's (1960) predictive failure test. The last test was applied by estimating over 1963-1982 and using these estimates to forcast over the period 1983-86.

The equations were estimated using Hashem Pesaran's DATA-FIT package.

Finally, the equations of Table 6.4 were tested for parameter stability by estimating them on data up to 1982 and using the estimates to generate static forecasts for the period 1983-6. (The result from these tests are shown in Table 6.4 under the column $\chi^2(4)$) Of the 7 equations only one – for Q5 appeared to have parameters that did not, on a χ^2 forecasting test, appear to be stable over time.

The estimated equations appear to be fairly well determined, characterised by high goodness-of-fit and correctly signed coefficient estimates, most of which are significantly different from zero. An examination of the detailed results however reveals certain interesting features. One interpretation of the coefficient on the error-correction term, $\log(c/y)_{t-1}$, is that it represents the marginal propensity to consume out of assets (see Deaton and Muellbauer (1980), p 335). On this interpretation the propensity to consume out of assets rises steadily from households in Q1 to those in Q4, falling only slightly for households in Q5. Another feature of the results is the fact that the impact effect of a rise in income on consumption is highest for households in Q1 and Q2 (with correspondingly low mean lags), [14] while for Q4 and Q5 the impact effect is relatively small and the mean lag relatively long. This again is highly plausible and accords well with the characteristics of the persons occupying these quintiles (cf. section 6.3).

Table 6.5
Long Run Properties of Equation (6.6)

Quintile	log K	1 - K (g = 0.025)
1	0.18-0.14g	-0.19
2	0.10-0.03g	-0.10
3	0.02-0.10g	-0.02
4	-0.04-0.23g	0.04
5	-0.11-0.41g	0.11
Aggregate (FES)	-0.02-0.45g	0.03
Aggregate (UKNA)	-0.047-1.04g	0.07

The long run properties are derived from the estimates shown in in Table 6.4.
g is the steady state rate of growth in real income.
1-K is the long run saving ratio when g = .025.

The long-run saving behaviour of the quintiles, shown in Table 6.5 also appears plausible. As noted above, with real income growing at a constant rate g, and with no price changes, equation (6.6) will yield a constant proportionality between consumption and income, though the coefficient of proportionality would vary inversely with g. On the assumption of a 2.5 per cent steady-state growth rate, the implied values of K – the long run consumption-income ratio – were 1.19, 1.10, 1.02, 0.96, 0.89 and 0.97 for the Q1-Q5 and the aggregate (FES) equations respectively. Thus the results imply that, in a steady state, households in the lower quintiles would be dissavers, with the bulk of saving coming from households in the top quintile. The facts accord well with our knowledge of inter-quintile differences in saving behaviour as evidenced by FES data (cf. section 6.3). The value of K = 0.97 for the aggregate (FES) equation for $\Delta \log c_t$ is consistent with K = 0.93 for the aggregate (UKNA) equation, with the long-run saving ratio being higher for the latter since it relates to the saving of the personal sector as a whole, rather than to the saving of only the household sector. Indeed a comparison of the aggregate equations based respectively on FES and UKNA data indicates that the two sets of estimates are not dissimilar. This serves to increase confidence in the quality of the quintile data constructed from the FES.

6.5 The Economic Implications of Redistributive Policies

In order to quantify the magnitude of income distribution changes on aggregate consumption three simulation experiments were conducted using the Davidson et al. (1978) model and its estimates shown in Table 6.4. The initial values for the simulations were the values for 1986. In this year, which was also the last year of the estimation sample, the proportions of aggregate disposable income accruing to households in quintiles 1-5 were 0.06, 0.11, 0.17, 0.24 and 0.42 respectively. It was assumed in all the simulations that aggregate real per household disposable income grew at an annual rate of 2.5 per cent over the period 1986-2000 and that the price level remained at its 1986 value. On the assumption that the quintile shares over this period were given by their 1986 values, the first simulation (the base run) compared the aggregate volume of real per household consumption and the implied saving ratio obtained by using the aggregate equation (equation (6) of Table 6.4) with the same aggregate, and the same ratio, obtained by aggregating over the individual quintile equations (equations (1-5) of Table 6.4). The two procedures led to very different conclusions, with the aggregate saving ratio converging to 3 per cent when it was obtained from the aggregate equation and to 11 per cent when it was obtained from the disaggregated equations.

Table 6.6
Simulation Results of the Model of Total Consumers' Expenditure

		$s_t = 1 - c_t/y_t$			
Year	y_t	Base run: aggregate equation	Base run: quintile equations	More inequality: quintile equations	Less inequality: quintile equations
1987	135.75	0.03	0.10	0.12	0.05
1990	146.19	0.03	0.11	0.12	0.06
2000	211.72	0.03	0.11	0.12	0.06

y_t is household real disposable income, £ per week, 1980 prices; it is assumed to grow at 2.5 per cent per annum; the income shares are as defined in the text; s_t is the saving ratio.

The next simulation involved "more inequality than 1986" with, within the context of a 2.5 per cent annual growth in aggregate, per household, real disposable income, the quintiles obtaining their shares according to the proportions 0.04, 0.09, 0.15, 0.26 and 0.46 for Q1-Q5 respectively. Under the changed income distribution assumptions, the "forecasts" from the aggregate equation of course remained unchanged from the base run. The "forecasts" obtained by aggregating over the quintile equations were, however, markedly different. The saving ratio over the simulation period at 12 per cent was consistently higher by one percentage point (see Table 6.6, column 5) than that prevailing under the "1986 inequality level" run. The results for a similar simulation but with "less inequality than 1986", with the quintile shares given by 0.08, 0.16, 0.20, 0.26 and 0.30, led to the significantly lower saving ratio of 6 per cent. Thus it would appear from the above simulations that the redistribution of income quite apart from its role in promoting "social justice" could usefully be regarded as an instrument of demand management policy, both because it was capable of changing the pattern of consumption expenditure but also because it was capable of influencing the total of such expenditure.

6.6 Conclusions

The analysis of the household sector's consumption behaviour in this paper represents an exercise at a level of disaggregation intermediate between the standard macroeconomic treatment of the household sector as a single behavioural unit and the standard microeconomic analysis of the individual household. Specifications of aggregate consumption functions play slight attention to the problems of employing a specification for the aggregate, which has only been shown to be plausible for the individual. This procedure becomes especially disconcerting when the lack of homogeneity within the household sector is recognised. At any time, the sector contains households at all stages of the life cycle and at many different levels of lifetime income. Moreover the composition of the sector does not remain fixed, either with regard to the proportions of households at different stages of the life cycle, or with regard to the proportions in different "permanent" income classes.

Perhaps the only legitimate method of dealing with these issues involves abandoning the idea of a single aggregate specification and letting the saving behaviour of the sector as a whole be explained as the outcome of an explicit aggregation of the saving behaviour of the individual households which make up the sector. In the absence of the detailed information that this would require, it seems reasonable to examine the possibility of intermediate levels of analyses such as attempted in this chapter. Here the unit of analysis is a group of households, much wider in scope than the individual household used in microeconomic analysis, but considerably narrower than the household sector in its entirety as used in macroeconomic analysis.

One of the main problems raised in the analysis of the chapter serves to suggest the principal areas where the approach needs development. This concerns the selection of the household groups. Given the frequency with which the absence of income distribution considerations is cited in the literature as a shortcoming of conventional consumption function studies, income classes are a natural choice. However, it is by no means clear how these classes are to be appropriately defined. Strict adherence to the life-cycle hypothesis suggests that households should be ranked with respect to lifetime resources, defined as current non-human net worth plus the present discounted value of current and expected future labour earnings. The corresponding "income" classes would be associated with the notions of the "permanently" poor and the "permanently" rich. On this basis, some of the notional households classified in this paper as "low income" might appear among the better off when their wealth holdings were taken into account. To determine the location of a particular household in this distribution, reference must thus be made not only to its current income, but also to its accumulated (and inherited) wealth and also to its expected future income stream.

There is very little data available on the joint distribution of households by current income and wealth (cf. Stark, 1978)). This alone makes a grouping of households by "lifetime income" empirically infeasible at the present time. If, however, such data were available and wealth effects could be included into the consumption functions of the ineome classes, then it might be that distributional considerations might emerge as even more important since now, in addition to the distribution of income, aggregate consumption would also be influenced by the distribution of wealth.

At the same time the "real world" behaviour of households may not warrant the use of saving models which adhere strictly to the life-cycle hypothesis. More myopic decision-making by households would justify the approach adopted in this chapter of grouping households by current-income. However, as the FES demonstrates, whether or not the life-cycle theory of saving is applicable, demographic life-cycle factors are clearly connected with current-income status. More work is needed on the implications of the life-cycle hypothesis for the distribution of current income in any year and the assignment of households at various stages of the cycle and in different "streams" of permanent income to the classes of the current-income distribution.

Finally, a major conclusion that would follow from the analysis of this chapter is that a policy of taxes and transfers that attempted to alter the distribution of a given economy-wide aggregate of disposable income between "rich" and "poor" households could change the aggregate volume of consumers' expenditure in the economy and thus have significant macroeconomic consequences. Discussions of macro-policy ignore distributional considerations and concentrate instead on instruments that influence aggregate consumption by altering aggregate income. If this chapter has any message, then it is that this too limited an approach and that considerations of income distribution can, and should provide a further dimension to considerations of macroeconomic outcomes. The next chapter argues that an alteration in consumption patterns, within the context of a given aggregate of consumers' expenditure, could also have profound macroeconomic consequences.

NOTES

[1] See for example Hendry (1974), Ball et al. (1975), Wall et al. (1975), Deaton (1977), Davidson et al. (1978), Hendry and Ungern-Sternberg (1981), Ungern-Sternberg (1981) Davidson and Hendry (1981), Davis (1982), Deaton (1983), Hendry (1983), Muellbauer (1983) and Pesaran and Evans (1984).

[2] The term "income distribution" is used in this chapter to mean the size distribution of income and not distribution by source of income. Townend (1976) is an example of a study which looks at the effect of the latter on aggregate consumption. As is shown in the next section, there is no necessary connection between the two distribution concepts.

[3] Simmons (1980) looks at the effect of income distribution in the context of expenditure systems. This study is not concerned with the allocation of expenditure and consequently is not restricted to the proportional saving function assumption employed by Simmons within a static framework.

[4] Thus for example Deaton (1977) and Pesaran and Evans (1984) use total expenditure, while Davidson et al. (1978) and Hendry and Ungern-Sternberg (1981) restrict themselves to non-durable expenditure.

[5] Which consists of: wages and salaries, self-employment income, imputed housing income, investment income, private pension and annuity income, social security benefits and other income.

[6] The Gini coefficient is an index of inequality such that a higher value for the coefficient implies a greater degree of inequality. With perfect equality, ie. with every quintile taking 20 per cent of income, the Gini coefficient takes the value unity; with perfect inequality, ie. with the top quinitle taking all of total income, it takes the value zero. See Atkinson (1975) for a discussion of inequality measures.

[7] See, *Economic Trends*, November 1983, "Effects of taxes and benefits on household income, 1982" and *Economic Trends*, November 1987, "The distribution of income in the UK, 1984/85".

[8] Defined as household saving as a proportion of household disposable income.

[9] The models successively "encompass" their precursors. (cf. Chapter 5 for details).

[10] However Patterson (1985) gives a structural interpretation to the intercept term when the dependent variable is non-durable consumption.

[11] G_t, rather than $\Delta \log G_t$, was also tried but with even less success.

[12] To allow for the fact that the number of households in the total sample, and hence in each quintile, varies over the sample period (with a corresponding variation over time in the information content of the quintiles) the observations for each year were weighted, prior to estimation, by the square root of the number of households for that year. The results however appeared to be very similar to those obtained from the unweighted observations (cf. Darrough, Pollack and Wales (1983)).

[13] The test was whether $\lambda=0$ in $\Delta\log(y + \lambda y^g) \cong \Delta\log y + \lambda\Delta(y^g/y)$. One would therefore introduce $\Delta(y^g/y)_t$ into the equation and test for a coefficient significantly different from zero.

[14] The mean lag is $(1-\beta)/(1-\alpha)$.

7. Income distribution, consumption patterns and economic outcomes

7.1 Introduction

The previous chapter pointed to the use of redistributive policies both as instruments to promote social cohesion and also as instruments to promote economic growth. The possibility that an effective anti-poverty policy (based upon an appropriate redistribution of income) could also be viewed as a credible economic policy was however commented upon there almost paranthetically. The time has come to pursue this topic more vigorously and that indeed is the purpose of this chapter.

There can be little doubt that, since 1979, when the first of three successive Conservative governments was elected, the distribution of income in the United Kingdom has become markedly more unequal. First, there has been a considerable improvement in the incomes of people fortunate enough to keep their jobs, vis-a-vis those who have become unemployed. Between 1979 and 1986, in manufacturing industry in the UK, post tax real earnings rose by almost 20 per cent, output fell by 9 per cent and employment fell by almost 26 per cent (Grahl and Rowthorn (1986)). As a consequence there has been a huge redistribution of income within the former manufacturing workforce, with some people gaining through higher wages, financed by higher productivity, but with others, who failed to hold on to their jobs, experiencing dramatic falls in income.

Secondly, even among persons in employment, there has been, since 1979, a considerable shift in income from the low paid to the high paid. The New Earnings Survey of 1986 illustrates the contrasting experiences of the different income groups. Since 1979, the highest paid 20 per cent of all male full-time workers enjoyed pay rises of 120 per cent. Over the same period, the bottom 20 per cent of male full-timers saw their pay rise by 87 per cent. (The median pay increase between 1979-86 for such workers was 100 per cent). As a consequence, in 1986, wages in the bottom quintile were only 65 per cent of the overall weekly average of £163, while the highest quintile earned 55 per cent more than the average. Exactly one hundred years ago, in 1886, the corresponding figures for the bottom and top quintiles were 69 and 43 per cent respectively (Smail 1986b).

Our own calculations based on FES data and detailed in the previous chapter in Figure 6.1 and Tables 6.2 and 6.3, have borne testimony to the growing income disparities in contemporary Britain. A consequence of growing income disparities, at a time of general recession, is the increasing numbers of persons living at or near poverty level. The Supplementary Benefit (SB) level of income is the level, specified by Parliament each year, below which the income of an individual or family, not in receipt of a wage for full-time employment, should not fall. [1] If the "poverty line" is defined as 140 per cent of SB income levels, (Townsend (1979), Mack and Lansley (1985)) then, in 1983, 16.38 million people, (30 per cent of the total population of Britain) could be regarded as "poor" (DHSS 1986). Latest estimates from the Low Pay Unit indicate that, in 1986, 18 million people (one-third of Britain's population) were living in a state of poverty (Smail 1986a) – an increase of 56 per cent over 1979 levels. [2]

In numerical terms poor people today constitute a significantly large proportion – ranging from a fifth to a third, depending upon ones definition of poverty – of Britain's population. As we have seen these numbers constitute a vast increase over 1979 levels. At this point it is appropriate therefore to ask who are the poor [3] and whether they are concentrated in particular subgroups of the population. The scale of the problem is certainly large enough to make the answer to such a query both politically and socially relevant.

The incidence of poverty, among households with a head unemployed for 3 months or more, has always been high; in 1979, 92 per cent of such households were poor. Next highest is the incidence of poverty among households with a head over pension age; in 1979, 68 per cent of such households were poor. These figures for incidence have not changed much over the past 8 years. What has changed however, is the **number** of households with unemployed heads. As a consequence the most important change over the period 1979-83 (1983 being the last year for which the DHSS published its detailed statistics on low income families) has been in the **composition** of the poor, with families with unemployed heads constituting a much greater proportion of the total population of poor families in 1983 than in 1979. (Atkinson, Hills and Le Grand (1987)).

There seems little doubt that the rise in the numbers unemployed, since Mrs Thatcher first came to power, has been associated with an increase in poverty. This rise has however affected different groups of the population differently. The people worst affected have been semi-skilled and unskilled workers and blacks, women and youths. To take two examples, in 1980-81, 51 per cent of long term unemployed men were either semi-skilled or unskilled (White (1983)); over the period 1979-86 male unemployment rose by 143 per cent, that for women by 189 per cent (Glendenning (1987)). In other words it is the economically most vulnerable sections of the population who have been worst hit by the recession.

Differences in the regional incidence of unemployment means that the poor are also concentrated geographically, with a large proportion of them living north of an imaginary line running from the Severn to the Wash. Thus the unemployment rate of 8.5 per cent prevailing in the South East in January 1987 was very low compared to the corresponding rate of 17 per cent for the North east. Not only was unemployment much higher in the "North" of Britain than in the "South" but the incidence of **long term** unemployment (i.e. persons out of work for over a year) was also much higher. As a consequence the average weekly household income in the "North" was, in 1986, two-thirds that in the "South".

7.2 Policies to Combat Poverty: The Equity-Efficiency Trade Off

In these circumstances, the urgent need for policies to arrest, if not to reverse this, seemingly inexorable, process of growing inequality and increasing poverty, has not escaped the attention of the main British political parties. Both the Social and Liberal Democrats and the Labour party include in their manifestos redistributive policies which, although differing in detail from each others, have the common aim of reducing poverty in contemporary Britain. However enthusiasm for such policies is moderated somewhat by anxiety about the possible loss of efficiency that their implementation might entail. It is an ingrained habit of economists to think in terms of a trade-off between equity and efficiency and it is this, no doubt, that underlies apprehensions about the deleterious effects of greater equality.

The massive scale of the "poverty problem" in Britain today has led some economists, however, to question the validity of this equity – efficiency trade off. One line of enquiry (Pahl (1984), Piachaud (1987)) has focussed on the increasing concentration of paid work that has occurred in the 1980s. Thus Pahl's (1984) study suggests that polarisation between "productive" and "unproductive" households is partly caused by the fact that households with members in employment are in the best position to find employment for other household members. As a consequence there is a great contrast between productive, busy households with money and unproductive, idle households without money. There is therefore, according to this analysis, an intimate connection between inefficiency, in the sense of limited employment opportunities, and inequality in the distribution of such opportunities.

These sentiments are echoed by Piachaud (1987) who deplores the "artificial division between goals of efficiency and of equity ... since in many cases efficiency and equity goals may correspond, not conflict" (p.60). Thus for example, in relation to unemployment, training and job guarantees may contribute to efficiency and to equity, as indeed may do a range of other social policies from making part-time work more flexible to increasing the provision of child care facilities. Similarly regional disparities should also be viewed from the point of view of the efficiency losses that occur when substantial parts of the country lack economic opportunities. An expansion of the set of available opportunities would thus succeed in promoting both efficiency and equity.

These criticisms of the efficiency-equity trade-off may be termed "supply side" criticisms since they focus on improving efficiency, by expanding the supply of opportunities, with greater equity following in the wake of this expansion. By way of contrast, this chapter mounts an assault on the efficiency-equity trade off from the point of view of demand. The argument here is precisely the opposite of that outlined above. It is that making income distribution more equitable – through appropriate redistributive measures – raises the level of aggregate consumer demand in the economy (see Chapter 6) and also alters its commodity composition. This in turn leads to higher rates of growth for the economy. In other words, more equality leads to greater efficiency.

The reasons for this sequence of events is straight forward. Firstly, by virtue of the fact that the "poor" have demonstratively higher propensities to consume than the "rich" a, reduction in income inequalities could serve to increase output and employment. This has been the theme of the previous chapter. Secondly, the consumption patterns of "poor" households will typically be markedly different from those of "rich" households; as a consequence their consumption responses (in terms of expenditure on the variety of available goods and services) to changes in income and relative prices should also be different.

A policy that altered the distribution of income between "poor" and "rich" households would therefore, in addition to altering the level of aggregate consumption demand in the economy, also alter the composition of such demand. A change in the composition of consumer demand would, in turn, have implications for the structure of industrial output. This would have a direct effect on the aggregate level of employment in the economy (since some industries are more labour intensive than others) but, also, these direct effects would be supplemented by indirect effects operating through the ensuing changes in the economy's balance of payments position. There is therefore, in summary, a plausible link between income distribution, aggregate demand, industrial change and macroeconomic outcomes. The aim of this chapter is to investigate the nature of this link for the UK economy.

The strategy for doing so was to first construct, using the Family Expenditure Survey (FES), data on quintile expenditure on 10 broad commodity groups and then to estimate, on such data, the Rotterdam model of consumers' expenditure discussed earlier in Chapter 3. This exercise is described in the next section, 7.3. Section 7.4 uses these estimates to construct a simulation model which, under different assumptions about redistributive policies, projects to the year 2000, the shares in the household budgets of the different commodity groups. Section 7.5 then feeds these budgetary changes into an industrially disaggregated model of the UK economy and thereby derives the macroeconomic implications of such changes. Section 7.6 then concludes the chapter.

7.3 Data and Estimation

The expenditure data used in this paper are taken from the published annual reports of the FES for the years 1963-86. The FES is the only regular source of UK data containing information on consumption behaviour by income group. Average household expenditure on goods and services is presented in these reports for households grouped into bands on the basis of "gross" income. For the purposes of this paper, 10 commodity groups are distinguished and they are: housing; fuel and power; food; alcohol; tobacco; footwear and clothing; durable household goods; "other" goods; transport and vehicles; services. The deficiences of the data are well known (Kensley, Redpath and Holmes (1980) Atkinson and Micklewright (1983) and need not detain us unduly; nor need much space be devoted to a description of the commodity groups which are defined in detail in the individual reports. [4]

Using these data, time series for expenditure, by quintile of gross weekly household income (denoted Q1 (lowest) to Q5 (highest)), were constructed for the period 1963-86 using linear interpolation on the standard published tables based on nominal income bands. The technique for doing so has been described in Chapter 6 but can, perhaps, bear repetition. The nominal income bands were amalgamated (and split where necessary) to give, each year, five bands ranked in ascending order of gross income, with 20 per cent of the total number of households in the sample allocated to each band. Errors in this procedure would arise when the published income bands straddled quintile endpoints. Of the income which accrued in aggregate to the households belonging to such a straddling band, the proportion allocated to the lower of the two quintiles was set equal to the fraction of the number of households in the band which were required to bring the cumulative proportion of households in the sample up to the multiple of 20 per cent which defined the endpoint between the two quintiles in question. The same proportion calculated in this way was used to allocate consumer expenditure on each of the 10 commodity groups. Some idea of the accuracy of this procedure may be obtained by a comparison of our data with data on disaggregated expenditure by quintile published by the FES since 1978. An examination of Table 7.1 which provides an itemised comparison for 1985 shows that the differences are indeed very slight.

Several differences in household consumption patterns across the quintiles are revealed in this Table. The budget share of fuel and power, food, tobacco and "other" goods falls with increasing household affluence; on the other hand budget shares for alcohol, footwear and clothing, household durables, transport and vehicles rises with greater affluence. The budget share for housing rises sharply from households in Q1 to households in Q2 and thereafter falls across the quintiles. This last phenomenon may not be unconnected with the characteristics of households in the different quintiles. Among households in the lowest quintile, the overwhelming majority of dwellings are rented, unfurnished, from local authorities; of the respondents in this quintile to the 1985 FES, 65 per cent lived in such dwellings. The next most popular form of tenure among households in this quintile, were dwellings owned outright (17 per cent of respondents). The preponderance of council house tenants in this quintile, in which the average age of the head of a household is 61 years, means that housing costs are low, though the quality of housing may be correspondingly poor. In the second quintile, the proportion of council house tenants falls sharply to 38 per cent and the average household size rises (from 1.49 persons in Q1) to 2.34 persons. A combination of both factors probably leads housing costs as a proportion of total expenditure to rise sharply. Thereafter the average household size increases but relatively slowly; housing costs rise but not as fast as total expenditure and its budget share falls.

Table 7.1
A Comparison of Expenditure at Current Prices, by Quintile, on 10 Commodity Groups, 1985

	Gross Weekly Household Income £ per week per household				
	Q1	Q2	Q3	Q4	Q5
Housing	8.00 (7.78)	19.57 (19.73)	26.10 (26.13)	32.67 (32.55)	43.70 (43.79)
Fuel and Power	7.45 (7.44)	9.28 (9.29)	9.57 (9.52)	10.43 (10.31)	13.05 (13.19)
Food	16.17 (16.13)	25.12 (25.06)	32.28 (32.33)	39.11 (39.00)	50.88 (50.96)
Alcohol	1.96 (1.93)	4.22 (4.15)	7.34 (7.40)	10.16 (10.15)	16.08 (16.09)
Tobacco	2.67 (2.68)	4.03 (4.00)	4.98 (4.95)	5.02 (4.86)	5.42 (5.60)
Footwear and Clothing	3.54 (3.49)	6.88 (6.89)	11.18 (11.17)	14.68 (14.46)	23.35 (23.58)
Household Durables	2.37 (2.44)	6.29 (6.00)	11.06 (11.33)	14.75 (14.48)	23.58 (23.57)
Other Goods	4.72 (4.78)	8.15 (8.07)	11.81 (11.77)	15.47 (15.26)	22.79 (23.03)
Transport and Vehicles	3.87 (3.87)	11.71 (11.73)	21.68 (21.72)	32.50 (32.26)	53.07 (53.21)
Services	5.98 (5.80)	11.31 (11.57)	16.00 (15.93)	21.65 (21.29)	42.47 (42.78)
Total	56.73 (56.40)	106.56 (106.54)	152.00 (152.30)	196.44 (194.67)	294.39 (296.03)

FES quintile data in parantheses; own estimates in line above.

The Rotterdam model of consumer demand (described in chapter 3) was estimated on this data set; for reasons of economy of space these estimates are not reproduced in this paper though they may be obtained on request from the author. At each stage of the estimation process, the validity of the restrictions implied by the theory of demand, viz. adding up, homogeneity, symmetry and negativity, were tested. Likelihood ratio tests showed however that, in common with the experience of other investigators in this area, the data rarely accepted the validity of such restrictions. [5] In fact it was only the property of homogeneity that could not be rejected (against the alternative of an unconstrained substitution matrix) and that also for only quintiles 2 and 4. The symmetry restrictions were never accepted, either by themselves against homogeneity or, together with homogeneity, against the unconstrained case.

The estimated expenditure elasticities, which form the basis for the subsequent simulations, are shown in Table 7.2. These are the estimates obtained by imposing the appropriate data-consistent restrictions; in view of the above discussion, they are mostly unconstrained estimates. The results demonstrate considerable differences between the consumption behaviour of households in the different quintiles. Households in the second quintile had the most even allocation of an increase in total expenditure across the commodity groups; the highest elasticity was 1.26 (alcohol) and the lowest was 0.77 (housing). Households in the third quintile also displayed a fairly even allocation with a highest elasticity of 1.60 (clothing and footwear) and a lowest of 0.39 (household durables). The other quintiles displayed more extreme behaviour: the poorest households had a very large elasticity for housing (3.64); the richest had a very large elasticity for household durables (4.37) while households in Q4 had large elasticitics for clothing and footwear (2.21) and household durables (2.04).

Table 7.2
Commodity Groups Expenditure Elasticities Estimated by Quintile

	Q1	Q2	Q3	Q4	Q5
Housing	3.64	0.77	0.84	0.19	0.41
Fuel and Power	0.54	0.78	1.40	0.40	0.45
Food	0.42	1.13	1.22	0.26	0.49
Alcohol	0.47	1.26	1.50	0.94	0.86
Tobacco	0.47	0.90	0.68	-0.85	0.25
Clothing and Footwear	0.23	1.00	1.60	2.21	0.48
Household Durables	0.86	1.16	0.39	2.04	4.37
Other Goods	0.14	1.02	0.80	1.05	1.06
Transport and Vehicles	1.93	1.21	0.75	1.95	1.16
Services	0.57	0.89	1.03	1.56	0.61

An inspection of Table 7.2 also makes it possible to separate many of the commodities into two groups: those for which "poor households" (in Q1 and Q2) have a higher elasticity than "rich households" (in Q4 and Q5) and those for which they do not. Belonging to the former category are housing, fuel and power, food and tobacco. Belonging to the latter category are household durables, clothing and footwear, other goods and services. The two remaining commodity groups, alcohol and transport and vehicles cannot be, unambiguously categorized. The category transport and vehicles itself covers a variety of items ranging from the purchase of motor vehicles to the buying of bus and coach tickets. It is likely that beneath the even spread of elasticities for this category across "poor" and "rich" households lie such compositional differences, with the expenditure of "poor" households being on coach, bus and rail fares and the expenditure of "rich households" being biased towards the purchase and maintenance of motor vehicles.

Several of the other commodity groups will, of course, also contain compositional differences; in the simulations that follow in the next sections an attempt will be made to take into account such differences by reference to the details of the FES. For the moment it suffices to note that, on the basis of the evidence of our estimates, there is *a priori* evidence that a change in the distribution of income will lead to a change in the pattern of consumers' expenditure. This will, as a consequence, affect the composition of industrial output which, in turn, will have implications both for the balance of payments and for employment. These matters are pursued more fully below.

7.4 Income Distribution and the Pattern of Consumers' Expenditure in the UK

Of total consumption expenditure in the UK in 1986, FES estimates show that about 7 per cent was by households in Q1, 13 per cent by households in Q2, 19 per cent by households in Q3, 24 per cent by households in Q4 and 37 per cent by households in Q5. There is therefore, in the UK, an inequality in the distribution of consumer goods and services, which reflects the prevailing inequality in the distribution of disposable incomes (see Table 6.3). The implications of altering this pattern of distribution of aggregate consumption, for the demands for the 10 commodity groups in the household budget, are explored in this section: [6] in the subsequent section the broader implications of such changes, in terms of their effects upon the economy, are examined.

In order to provide this wider perspective, it was necessary to embed the model of consumers' expenditure, estimated in this paper, within a model of the entire economy. The only such model, for the UK, which is also disaggregated by industry, is the Cambridge Growth Project's (CGP) model. [7] It is within the context of this model, that the simulation exercises, described in this section and the next, were carried out. The starting point of the simulations was the projection of aggregate real consumers' expenditure (ARE) in the UK, for the period 1986-2000, provided by the CGP model. For 1986, the starting year of the simulations, ARE [8] was divided between the quintiles, according to the consumption shares prevailing, to yield the aggregate real consumption expenditures of the quintiles (QRE). Using the 1986 budget shares from the FES report, the 5 component vector QRE, was split between the 10 commodity groups used in this paper, to yield, for 1986, the 5 x 10 matrix of quintile commodity group expenditures (CGE).

From this starting position, two simulations were carried out. The first, Simulation A, was the "no change" simulation, in which the shares of the quintiles in ARE, were held, over the simulation period 1987-2000, at their 1986 values. This simulation effectively provided the benchmark against which the next simulation, Simulation B, could be evaluated. This was one in which it was assumed that redistributive policies would be followed which would reduce the degree of income inequality and, ipso facto, the degree of consumption inequality. Under Simulation B therefore, the quintile shares in ARE became progressively less unequal (relative to 1986) over the 3 year period, 1987-89, and then stayed at their 1989 values (of 10, 19, 20, 22 and 29 per cent for Q1 – Q5 respectively) for the remainder of the simulation period. [9]

The manner in which these simulations were carried out was as follows. For 1986, as already described, one had values for the elements of the vector QRE and the matrix CGE. For the subsequent years, 1987-2000 one could compute values for QRE, where of course these values depended on the CGP model's projection for ARE in (say) 1987 and also on the choice of simulations between A and B. Given the 1987 value for QRE, the values, for 1987, for the elements of the matrix CGE were computed by using the estimated expenditure elasticities [10] for the commodity groups (see Table 7.2) to allocate changes in total quintile expenditure, QRE, across changes in quintile expenditure on the 10 commodity groups, CGE.

The budget shares of the 10 commodity groups, for the aggregate of households over the quintiles, are shown in Table 7.3, for the two simulations, for their starting (1987) and finishing (2000) years. Although the budget shares, **within** each simulation, stabilised from about 1993 onwards, there were considerable differences in these shares, **between** the simulations. [11] By the year 2000, the budget share of food was 3 percentage points higher under Simulation B; that of housing was higher by 2 percentage points and of household durables was lower by 3 percentage points. If one bears in mind that these changes had, in fact, come into effect by the early 1990s, then the effect of redistributive policies on the

Table 7.3
Aggregate Budget Shares in 1986 and 2000 for the 10 Commodity Groups (%)

	Simulation A		Simulation B	
Housing	15.85	(14.93)	16.49	(16.92)
Fuel and Power	6.13	(5.78)	6.28	(6.29)
Food	20.31	(19.04)	20.76	(20.53)
Alcohol	4.84	(4.72)	4.82	(4.65)
Tobacco	2.77	(2.47)	2.88	(2.80)
Clothing and Footwear	7.42	(7.63)	7.33	(7.55)
Household Durables	7.82	(10.00)	7.09	(7.25)
Other Goods	7.81	(7.71)	7.73	(7.45)
Transport and Vehicles	15.28	(16.14)	14.96	(15.16)
Services	11.77	(11.58)	11.67	(11.40)

Values for the year 2000 in parantheses.

pattern of commodity demands in the UK would appear to be profound. The effect of these changes on the economy as a whole is the topic of the next section.

7.5 Changes in Consumption Patterns and Economic Outcomes in the UK

The results of this section were obtained by embedding the consumption model, developed in this chapter in terms of 10 broad commodity groups, within the CGP model of the UK economy. This then enabled the broader economic implications of changes in income distribution and consumption patterns to be deduced. The CGP model however operated in terms of a 49 category commodity classification, of which expenditure on only 4 did not concern households, but concerned rather only the institutional subsector.s within the personal sector [12] In order to use the CGP model it was necessary therefore to reduce the 10 commodity groups, employed so far, to the 45 commodity classification of the model.

This was achieved by subdividing each of the 10 broad groups into a narrower set of commodities thus resulting in a 5 x 45 matrix, CE,the typical element of which represented expenditure by quintile i(i= 1...5) on commodity j(j=1...45). [13] The budget share of each commodity in its commodity group was calculated for 1986, for each quintile, from the FES report; in the simulations it was assumed that, while the values of CGE changed from year to year, the values of the elements of CE, the commodity matrix, were obtained by applying to the relevant element of CGE, the constant (1986) budget shares. (Thus for example, the broad group food was subdivided into 11 commodities (see note 13 for details). In 1986, the share of meat and bacon in the food budget was 22, 24, 22, 20 and 19 per cent for Ql, Q2, Q3, Q4, and Q5 respectively. Although, in the simulations, the food budget changed over time, the share of meat and bacon, in the food budget of each quintile, was assumed constant at its 1986 value and the value of expenditure on meat and bacon, by each quintile, was obtained by applying these constant budget shares to its overall food budget).

In this manner, real commodity demand, by quintile, for each of the 45 commodities was calculated for each year of the simulation period, 1987-2000 for simulations A and B. Adding the demands over the quintiles, then yielded, for each year, and each simulation, a 45 component vector of real aggregate commodity demand (ACE). Dividing the values of ACE under simulation B, by its values under Simulation A, then yielded for each year, the vector of relative, proportionate changes induced by a policy of promoting "less inequality", over the "no change" position. As was to be expected, these changes were in consonance with the results of Table 7.3.

By 2000, there were increases in the demand for all food items (on average 10 per cent higher under the more egalitarian policies), coal and coke (16 per cent higher), rent and rates (15 per cent higher), tobacco (14 per cent higher), bus and coach travel (11 per cent higher) and maintenance of dwellings (6 per cent higher). This was balanced by [14] falls in the demand for furniture and floor coverings (32 per cent lower), other durables (25 per cent lower), insurance on the contents of dwellings (32 per cent lower), rail travel (11 percent lower), motor vehicles (10 per cent lower), expenditure abroad (5 per cent lower) and wines and spirits (4 per cent lower).

These changes were then inserted into the "base" run of the CGP model [15] by modifying the existing commodity demand vector in the "base" CGP run to incorporate the changes, the most important of which were noted above. [16] This run was labelled the "new" run. To begin with, in both the runs, the total of commodity demands was the same, namely that of the "base" run. Thus the only respect in which the runs initially differed was in their pattern of commodity demands; the "new" run was based on a pattern of demand which was a consequence of more egalitarian policies being pursued. However because the pattern of demand were different between the two runs, they eventually, from the same starting position, yielded very different economic outcomes. These differences are explored below.

Changes in consumption patterns impinge on the composition of industrial outputs. The CGP model distinguishes 40 different industries; by the end of the simulation period, output of agriculture and of the food manufacturing, tobacco, construction, coal, gas, water, electricity and "other vehicles" industries was higher than under "base" and output of the engineering industries, of the metal manufacturing industries and of motor vehicles was significantly lower. Since the latter group of industries had significantly higher import penetration ratios [17] than the former group, the total volume of imports under the "new" run was about 82 per cent of that under the "base" run; the fall in exports was less severe (only 95 per cent of "base") and, as a consequence, the balance of payments position in 2000 was much healthier under the "new" run.

The macroeconomic consequences of these shifts in the composition of industrial outputs are detailed in Table 7.4 at four yearly intervals, beginning with 1987. As is evident, real GDP growth is consistently higher under the more egalitarian policies with the impetus for growth coming partly from real consumption growth and partly from a slower rate of growth in import volumes; conversely, under the same set of policies, GDP growth is checked by a slower rate of growth in real capital formation and export volumes.

Paradoxically, inspite of higher output growth, the "new" run offers poorer prospects for employment than the "base" run. Table 7.5 shows that by 2000, employment under the former simulation is lower, relative to the "base" run, by just over 2 million persons. The resolution of this paradox is not difficult – it lies in differential productivity levels and growth across industries and also in movements in the exchange rate. The time path of the dollar/sterling exchange rate under the two simulations is shown in Table 7.5; it is clear that the healthier balance of payments position under the "new" run also leads to sterling being stronger under this run. The consequences of this are essentially two: exports are lower under the more egalitarian policies and this in turn affects employment; the same set of policies result in a lower inflation rate and higher real wage growth. Growth in real wages boosts consumer spending and this goes some way to counteracting the employment effects of lower exports.

Table 7.4
Macroeconomic Outcomes Under the "New" and "Base" Runs

	Annual Growth Rates (%)				
	GDP	C	IK	M	X
1987	2.2 (2.2)	3.5 (3.3)	3.4 (3.3)	4.5 (4.4)	2.4 (2.5)
1990	1.9 (1.3)	2.2 (1.3)	3.3 (3.5)	2.9 (3.5)	2.7 (3.0)
1994	2.4 (1.8)	2.1 (1.2)	3.1 (3.5)	2.7 (3.4)	3.6 (3.9)
1998	2.2 (1.6)	2.1 (1.2)	2.2 (2.8)	2.1 (3.0)	3.0 (3.4)
2000	2.3 (1.9)	2.0 (1.2)	2.1 (2.8)	2.0 (2.8)	3.1 (3.6)

Notes: GDP = gross domestic product at market prices
C = consumers' expenditure
IK = gross domestic fixed capital formation
M = total imports of goods and services
X = total exports of goods and services
All variables are in constant prices; Base run figures in parantheses.

Differential productivity growth across industries, however, provide a further squeeze on employment. If one examines the industries whose outputs are raised and those whose outputs are reduced by the different consumption pattern of the "new" run (relative to the "base" run), then one finds that, in general, the former set of industries, have both higher productivity levels than the latter set and also exhibit higher growth rates in productivity. Table 7.6 attempts to convey the flavour of this argument by setting out productivity growth rates for a selected sample of industries: the first six of these are those whose outputs are higher under the "new" run and the last six are those whose output is lower. The differential pattern of productivity growth across the industries is abundantly clear from this Table and needs no further elaboration.

The above discussion involved a comparison between the two simulations on specific economic issues and from this it would appear that a greater degree of equality in Britain's economic life holds out the prospect of higher output and real wage growth in conjunction with a stronger pound and a lower rate of inflation but at the cost of a lower level of employment. The comparison was however based on the assumption that the two runs differed initially only with respect to their consumption patterns and that, in all other respects, they were identical. The time has come to question the validity of this assumption and, in particular, that aspect that held the levels of the policy instruments unchanged between the runs.

Conventional wisdom has it that the main constraint to reflationary policies of the broadly Keynesian type is the balance of payments and that, for a small, open economy like that of the UK, this constraint is, particularly onerous. In this context, the most striking feature of the run incorporating a less unequal division of the consumption cake, is the extent to which it frees the economy, through a sharp fall in its imports bill, from this constraint. In our

Table 7.5
Employment, Inflation, the Exchange Rate and Real Wages Under the "New" and "Base" Runs

	EM	IR	XR	RW
1986	24.1 (24.1)	2.39 (2.33)	1.43 (1.43)	4.59 (4.55)
1990	24.5 (24.9)	4.51 (5.36)	1.35 (1.31)	1.79 (1.79)
1994	24.2 (25.2)	5.49 (6.68)	1.31 (1.21)	1.23 (1.12)
1998	24.0 (25.7)	4.59 (6.19)	1.35 (1.15)	1.40 (1.30)
2000	23.7 (25.9)	4.41 (6.13)	1.40 (1.12)	1.66 (1.47)

Notes: EM = total employment, millions.
IR = annual rate of change in home unit costs, percentage.
XR = $/£ exchange rate.
RW = annual rate of growth in real wages, percentage
Base values in parantheses.

Table 7.6
Productivity in Selected Industries: "Base" Run Projections

	Output per Person	Growth in Output per Person, Annual % Change			
	1986	1990	1994	1998	2000
Agriculture	12.16(6)	5.07	3.62	3.44	3.34
Food Manufacturing	24.52(3)	2.39	2.81	2.99	3.22
Tobacco	31.60(2)	7.02	7.70	7.77	7.76
Construction	10.59(6)	1.57	2.17	1.47	1.91
Electricity	35.39(1)	7.07	2.01	0.97	0.73
Gas	21.17(4)	5.04	2.01	0.80	0.04
Technical Engineering	8.85(5)	0.91	0.77	0.70	0.88
Instrument Engineering	9.80(4)	5.50	5.68	3.98	4.42
Electrical Engineering	2.40(3)	4.54	2.73	-0.04	3.12
Motor Vehicles	15.12(2)	3.43	7.21	6.78	7.05
Iron and Steel	21.56(1)	-0.74	2.90	3.92	1.93
Professional Services	4.42(6)	1.07	1.76	3.51	3.37

Source: CGP base run.

simulation, the government, by allowing the exchange rate to appreciate sharply and by also maintaining public expenditure at an unchanged level (relative to "base"), does not take advantage of this relative freedom. But there is, of course, no reason why it should suffer from such inhibitions; indeed a bolder government might reduce interest rates, thereby promoting both investment and exports and also expand its expenditure. The upshot would be a rise in employment. Of equal importance is the fact that freedom from the straightjacket of the balance of payments would provide a valuable opportunity for the government to direct its spending towards a restructuring of the economy with a view to making it more competitive. Seen in this light, equality is not the enemy of efficiency, but rather its ally.

7.6 Conclusions

The role of consumption patterns in promoting economic development has exercised the minds of economists and other social scientists concerned with the affairs of less developed countries (Prebisch (1984)). In the developed world however, it has generally been assumed that the fruits of industrialisation were available to all its inhabitants; the problem in such a setting was therefore one of sustaining, and promoting, affluence rather than rescuing people from poverty. Contemporary Britain however provides evidence that, even in the midst of plenty, the scale and extent of poverty is, without exaggeration, quite alarming.

This chapter has tried to outline the economic logic of an anti-poverty policy. The main element of such a policy would be a more equal distribution of income. This would take the form of greater equality in both **pre-tax** and **post-tax** incomes. As we have seen, a feature of the Thatcher years has been a deliberate erosion in the economic position of the low paid (with a corresponding enhancement in the earnings of the well off). This has been based on the belief that the poor do not work because they have too much income and that the rich do not work because they do not have enough income. The policies that led to such an erosion – cuts in employment rights, abolition of wages councils, reductions in minimum wages – need, in the first instance, to be reversed.

As regards post-tax incomes the point that needs to be emphasised is that, of the total volume of tax cuts offered by Mrs Thatcher's governments between 1979 and 1987, 15 per cent accrued to tax payers with incomes over £50,000 a year. Such tax payers, constituting only 0.7 per cent of all tax payers, received an average tax cut of £219 per week. At the other end of the spectrum 3.2 million tax payers with incomes below £5,000 a year, constituting one-sixth of all tax payers, received an average tax cut of £1.85 per week. A fairer redistribution of post tax incomes does **not** mean higher taxes for all. It does mean a restructuring of the present system of income tax rates and allowances so as to yield a fairer distribution of existing tax benefits. The number of potential beneficiaries is so large (and the number of potential losers so small) that there are valuable political points to be scored through such redistribution.

But the most important point of a redistribution of income is that it would not be undertaken as an act of charity but rather as an instrument of economic policy. For too long people who have pressed for more egalitarian economic and social policies, have been held in check by the threatened loss of economic efficiency that such policies might entail. There is some evidence however that the credibility of this threat is weakening. Recent work by Pahl (1984) and Piachaud (1987) has attempted to show that greater efficiency, in the sense of an expansion of job opportunities, can lead to greater equality in the distribution of jobs. This chapter has also attempted to show that equity and efficiency can, and do, move in tandem, though the explanation adopted is different from earlier studies. The explanation in this chapter runs from greater equity in income distribution leading to both a higher aggregate of consumption and to a change in consumption patterns. The result is higher output and faster growth with considerably greater latitude for government to follow policies of demand management and structural change.

It is this realisation that growth and equity can, do, and must move in tandem that provides the key to an **effective** anti-poverty policy. By this is meant not policies of the traditional type which try to do "something" for the poor for reasons of altruism but which, at the same time, keep an eye on the possible economic losses that they might entail. Such "socially" motivated policies, though of immense importance, cannot by themselves solve the poverty problem. First, by implicitly acquiesing to the view that growth and equity are mutually antagonistic, they are essentially defensive policies. This then prevents them from being tied to an overall economic strategy and, in turn, leads to their second defect, namely that they smack too often of handouts to the poor. An effective anti-poverty policy must, be an attacking policy. This requires tying such a policy to an overall economic strategy for promoting growth in output and employment. The aim of this chapter has been to try and forge such a link.

NOTES

[1] From April 1987, the weekly rates of SB were as follows:

	SB (£) Ordinary Rate		SB (£) Long Term Rate
Single person	30.40		38.65
Couple	49.35		61.85
Child 0-10		10.40	
11-15		15.60	

[2] If the "poverty line" were defined as the SB level of income then there were, in 1979 and 1986, 6.07 and 10.43 million persons respectively, living in poverty – an increase of 72 per cent over the 7 year period. The number of SB recipients in 1987 was slightly under 5 million. The figures quoted includes members of recipients families. Over this same period the government raised the real value of SB by only 5 per cent. It is therefore extremely unlikely that this modest raising of the "poverty line" over 1979-87 could account for the massive increase in the numbers living in poverty.

[3] Defined as those with incomes at or below 140 per cent of SB.

[4] Though the following points could perhaps be usefully made: (i) housing expenditure consists of expenditure on rent (with an imputation for owner-occupied dwellings), rates, repairs and maintenance, (ii) expenditure on durable household goods excludes rental charges on audio-visual equipment but includes repairs as well as insurance payments on dwelling contents, (iii) expenditure on transport and vehicles includes the purchase of motor vehicles (as well as their spares and accessories) and the maintenance and running costs of such vehicles, (iv) the FES consistently understates (in comparison to the (UKNA) expenditure on alcohol and tobacco. (See UK Central Statistical Office, "FES/Blue Book expenditure comparisons for 1970-75" (available on request from the CS0).

[5] See however Chapter 3 on the importance of a sufficiently fine commodity disaggregation in satisfying the restrictions of demand theory.

[6] Such alterations will of course be effected by alterations, through changes in taxes and transfers, to the distribution of disposable income. The relationship between changes in income distribution and changes in the distribution of aggregate consumption expenditure is discussed in Chapter 6.

[7] See Barker and Peterson (1987) for details of the model.

[8] For 1986, the "projected" value is of course the UKNA value.

[9] The precise time path was:

	Q1	Q2	Q3	Q4	Q5
1986	7	13	19	24	37
1987	8	15	19	23	35
1988	9	17	19	22	33
1989-2000	10	19	20	22	29

[10] Note that the elasticities are time variant (see Chapter 3).

[11] A "more inequality" simulation (along the lines of Simulation B) A in which the Quintile shares, by 1989, were 6, 9, 15, 27 and 43 per cent respectively was also carried out. There was not much difference between the results of this simulation and those of Simulation A.

[12] Non profit making bodies, pension funds and the life funds of life assurance companies.

[13] The subdivision was as follows: Housing – rent and rates; maintenance. Fuel and Power – gas; electricity; coal and coke; other fuels. Food – bread and cereals; meat and bacon; fish; oils and fats; sugar, preserves, etc; dairy products; fruit; potatoes and vegetables; beverages; other manufactured food; catering. Alcohol – beer; wines and spirits. Tobacco – no subdivision. Clothing and footwear – clothing; footwear. Household durables – furniture and floor covering; textiles and soft furnishings; hardware; insurance; other durables. Other goods – matches, soap, etc.; books; newspapers; magazines, chemists goods; miscellaneous recreation goods; other miscellaneous goods. Transport and vehicles – purchase of motor vehicles; running costs of motor vehicles; rail travel; bus and coach travel; other travel. Services – postal services; telephone and telegraph services; entertainment; domestic service; expenditure abroad; other services.

[14] Remembering that under both simulations, the value of aggregate real consumption expenditure (ARE) was the same.

[15] This is the run which produces the Project's (most recent) economic forecast.

[16] Thus if, for example, the demand for bus travel in the "base" run was £X at constant prices, demand in the "new" run for bus travel would be £(1.11)x.

[17] This is defined as the ratio of imported output to domestic output. The CGP model provides forecasts of import penetration ratios by industry. For electrical engineering this was as high as 96 per cent and averaged over 50 per cent for the other engineering industries; conversely for the group whose output was higher in the new run, the highest import penetration ratio was for the food manufacturing industry (15 per cent).

References

Ando, A. and F. Modigliani (1963), 'The Life Cycle Hypothesis of Saving: Aggregate Implications and Tests', *American Economic Review*, vol. 53, pp. 55-84.

Atkinson, A.B. (1975), *The Economics of Inequality*, Clarendon Press, Oxford.

Atkinson, A.B. and J. Micklewright (1983) 'On the Reliability of Income Data in the Family Expenditure Survey 1970-77', *Journal of the Royal Statistical Society*, Series A, vol. 146, Part I, pp. 33-61.

Atkinson, A.B., J. Hills and J. Le Grand (1987) 'The Welfare State', in R. Dornbusch and R. Layard (ed) *The Performance of the British Economy*, Oxford University Press, Oxford.

Armstrong, A. (1979), 'An Analysis of Personal Saving in the UK', *The Manchester School*, vol. 47, pp. 369-90.

Armstrong, A. (1984), 'Personal Saving, Household Saving and Inflation', Department of Economics Discussion Paper, no. 84/153, University of Bristol, Bristol.

Baldwin, M.A., H. Hadid and G.D.A. Philips (1983), 'The Estimation and Testing of a System of Demand Equations for the UK', *Applied Economics*, vol. 15, pp. 81-90

Ball, R.J., B.D. Boatwright, T. Burns, P.W.M. Lobban and G.W. Miller (1975), 'The London Business School Quarterly Econometric Model of the U.K. Economy', in G.A. Renton (ed), *Modelling the Economy*, Heinemann, London.

Barker, T. S. and W. Peterson, (ed), (1987), *The Cambridge Multi-sectoral Dynamic Model of the British Economy*, Cambridge University Press, Cambridge.

Barten, A.P. (1966), *Therie en empire van een volledig stelsel van vraaguergelijkingen*, Doctoral dissertation, University of Rotterdam, Rotterdam.

Barten, A.P. (1969), 'Maximum Likelihood Estimation of a Complete System of Demand Equations', *European Economic Review*, vol. 1, pp. 7-73.

Bean, C.R. (1985), 'The Estimation of 'Surprise' Models and the 'Surprise' Consumption Function', Centre for Economic Policy Research, Discussion Paper no. 54, London.

Bera, A.K. and C.M. Jarque (1981), 'An efficient large sample test for normality of observations and regression residuals', *Australian National University Working Papers in Econometrics, no. 40*, Canberra.

Blinder, A.S. (1975), 'Distribution Effects and the Aggregate Consumption Function', *Journal of Political Economy*, vol. 83, pp. 447-75.

Blundell, R.W. (1988), 'Consumer Economics: Theory and Empirical Evidence - A Survey', *Economic Journal*, vol. 98, pp. 16-65.

Borooah, V.K. (1978), *An Econometric Model of the Personal Sector in the United Kingdom*, Ph.D. thesis, University of Southampton, Southampton

Borooah, V.K. (1985), 'Consumer Expenditure Estimates Using the Rotterdam Model: an application to the UK, 1954-81', *Applied Economics*, vol. 17, pp. 675-88.

Byron, R.P. (1970), 'The Restricted Aitken Estimation of Sets of Demand Relations', *Econometrica*, vol. 38, pp. 816-30.

Calder, J.R. (1978), 'The Stock of Consumer Durables in the United Kingdom', *Economic Trends*, no. 293, pp. 111-24.

Chow, G.C. (1960), 'Tests of Equality Between Sets of Coefficients in Two Linear Regressions', *Econometrica*, vol. 26, pp. 591-605.

Christensen, L.R., D.W. Jorgenson and L.J. Lau (1975), 'Transcendental Logarithmic Utility Functions', *American Economic Review*, vol. 65, pp. 367-83.

Cuthbertson, K. (1982), 'The Measurement and Behaviour of the UK Saving Ratio in the 1970's', *National Institute of Economic and Social Research Review*, no. 99, pp. 75-84.

Darrough, M.N., R.A. Pollack and T.J. Wales (1983), 'Dynamic and Stochastic Structure: An Analysis of Three Time Series of Household Budget Studies', *Review of Economics and Statistics*, vol. 65, pp. 274-81.

Davidson, J.E.H., D.F. Hendry, F. Srba and S. Yeo (1978), 'Econometric Modelling of the Aggregate Time-Series Relationships Between Consumers' Expenditure and Income in the United Kingdom', *Economic Journal*, vol. 88, pp. 661-92.

Davidson, J.E.H. and D.F. Hendry (1981), 'Interpreting Econometric Evidence: The Behaviour of Consumers' Expenditure in the UK.', *European Economic Review*, vol. 15, pp. 177-92.

Davis, E.P. (1982), The Consumption Function in Macroeconomic Models: A Comparative Study, *Bank of England Discussion Papers (Technical Series), no. 1*, London.

Davis, E.P. and I.D. Saville (1982), 'Mortgage Lending and the Housing Market', *Bank of England Quarterly Bulletin*, vol. 22, pp. 390-98.

Deaton, A.S. (1976), 'Personal Consumption', in T.S. Barker (ed) *Economic Structure and Policy*, Chapman and Hall, London.

Deaton, A.S. (1977), 'Involuntary Saving Through Unanticipated Inflation', *American Economic Review*, vol. 67, pp. 899-910.

Deaton, A.S. and J. Muellbauer (1979), 'An Almost Ideal Demand System', *American Economic Review*, vol. 70, pp. 312-26.

Deaton, A.S. and J. Muellbauer (1980), *Economics and Consumer Behaviour*, Cambridge University Press, Cambridge.

Deaton, A.S. (1983), 'Savings and Inflation: Theory and British Evidence', in F. Modigliani and R. Hemming (ed), *The Determinants of National Saving and Wealth*, Macmillan, London.

Debreu, G. (1954), 'Representation of a Preference Ordering by a Numerical Function', in R.M. Thrall (ed) *Decision Processes*, John Wiley, New York.

Debreu, G. (1959), *Theory of Value*, John Wiley, New York.

DHSS (1986), *Low Income Families - 1983*, Department of Health and Social Security, London.

Diewert, W.E. (1982), 'Duality Approaches to Microeconomic Analysis', in K.J. Arrow and M.D. Intrilligator (ed), *Handbook of Mathematical Economics*, vol. II. North Holland.

Doorn, J.V. (1975), 'Aggregate Consumption and the Distribution of Income', *European Economic Review*, vol. 6, pp. 417-23.

Edgeworth, F.Y. (1981), *Mathematical Psychics*, Kegan Paul, London.

Fisher, I. (1892), 'Mathematical Investigations in the Theory of Value and Prices', *Transactions of the Connecticut Academy of Arts and Sciences*, vol. 9, pp. 1-124.

Flavin, M. (1981), 'The Adjustment of Consumption to Changing Expectations about Future Income', *Journal of Political Economy*, vol. 89, pp. 974-1009.

Friedman, M. (1957), *A Theory of the Consumption Function*, Princeton University Press, Princeton, New Jersey.

Garganas, N.C. (1975) 'An Analysis of Consumer Credit and its Effects on the Purchase of Consumer Durables', in G.A. Renton (ed), *Modelling the Economy*, Heinemann, London.

Glendenning, C. (1987) 'Impoverishing Women', in A. Walker and C Walker (ed) *The Growing Divide: a social audit, 1979-87*, Child Poverty Action Group, London.

Godfrey, L.G. (1978), 'Testing Against General Autoregressive and Moving Average Error Models when the Regressors Include Lagged Dependent Variables', *Econometrica*, vol. 46, pp. 1293-302.

Gorman, W.M. (1959), 'Separable Utility and Aggregation', *Econometrica*, vol. 27, pp. 469-81.

Grahl, J. and Rowthorn, R. E. (1986), 'Dodging the Tax Questions', *Marxism Today*, vol. 30, no. 10, pp. 24-8.

Hall, R.E. (1978), 'Stochastic Implications of the Life Cycle Permanent Income Hypothesis', *Journal of Political Economy*, vol. 86, pp. 971-87.

Hendry, D.F. (1974), 'Stochastic Specification in an Aggregate Demand Model of the United Kingdom', *Econometrica*, vol. 42, pp. 559-78.

Hendry, D.F. and T. von Ungern-Sternberg (1981), 'Liquidity and Inflation Effects on Consumers' Expenditure', in A.S. Deaton (ed) *Essays in the Theory and Measurement of Consumer Behaviour in Honour of Sir Richard Stone*, Cambridge University Press, Cambridge.

Hendry, D.F. (1983), 'Econometric Modelling: The 'Consumption Function' in Retrospect', *Scottish Journal of Political Economy*, vol. 30, pp. 193-220.

Hicks, J.R. (1939), *Value and Capital*, Oxford University Press, Oxford.

Hurwicz, L. and H. Uzawa (1971), 'On the Integrability of Demand Functions', in J.S. Chipman, L. Hurwicz, M.K. Richter and M.F. Sonnenschein (ed), *Preferences, Utility and Demand*, Harcourt Brace Jovanovitch, New York.

Jones, T. (1981), 'The Household Sector', *Economic Trends*, no. 335, pp. 105-20.

Kensley, W.F.F., R.U Redpath, and M. Holmes, (1980), *Family Expenditure Survey Handbook*, H.M.S.O., London.

Keynes, J.M. (1936), *The General Theory of Employment, Interest and Money*, Macmillan, London.

Mack, J. and S. Lansley, (1985), *Poor Britain*, Allen and Unwin, London.

Modigliani, F. and R. Brumberg (1954), 'Utility Analysis and the Consumption Function: An Interpretation of Cross Section Data', in K. Kurihara (ed), *Post-Keynesian Economics*, Rutgers University Press, New Brunswick, New Jersey.

Moyle, J. and D.J. Reid (1975), 'Private Non-Profit Making Bodies Serving Persons', *Economic Trends*, no. 259, pp. 78-86.

Muellbauer, J. (1983), 'Surprises in the Consumption Function', *Economic Journal* (Supplement), pp. 34-50.

Pahl, R.R. (1984), *Divisions of Labour*, Basil Blackwell, Oxford.

Pareto, V. (1896), *Cours d'economie politique*, Rouge, Lausanne.

Patterson, K.D. (1985), 'Income Adjustments and the Role of Consumers' Durables in Some Leading Consumption Functions', *Economic Journal*, vol. 95, pp. 469-79.

Pesaran, M.H. and R.A. Evans (1984), 'Inflation, Capital Gains and UK Personal Savings: 1953-81', *Economic Journal*, vol. 94, pp. 237-57.

Piachaud, D. (1974), *Do the poor pay more?*, Child Poverty Action Group, Poverty Research Series, no. 3, London.

Piachaud, D. (1987). 'The Distribution of Income and Work', *Oxford Review of Economic Policy*, vol. 3, pp. 41-61.

Ramsey, J.B. (1969), 'Tests for Specification Errors in Classical Linear Least Squares Analysis', *Journal of the Royal Statistical Society*, Series B, vol. 31, pp. 350-71.

Prebisch, R. (1984), 'Five Stages in My Thinking on Development' in G. M. Meier and D. Seers (ed) *Pioneers in Development*, Oxford University Press, Oxford.

Royal Commission on the Distribution of Income and Wealth (1975), *Report No. 1*, HMSO, London.

Salmon, M. (1982), 'Error Correction Mechanisms', *Economic Journal*, vol. 92, pp. 615-29.

Samuelson, P.A. (1947), *Foundations of Economic Analysis*, Harvard University Press, Massachusetts.

Sen, A.K. (1979), 'Rational Fools: A Critique of the Behavioural Foundations of Economic Theory', in F. Hahn and M. Hollis (ed) *Philosophy and Economic Theory*, Oxford University Press, Oxford.

Simmons, P. (1980) 'Evidence on the Impact of Income Distribution on Consumer Demand in the UK, 1955-68', *Review of Economic Studies*, vol. 67, pp. 893-906.

Slutsky, E. (1915), 'On the Theory of the Budget of the Consumer', in G.J. Stigler and K.E. Boulding (ed) *Readings in Price Theory*, R.D. Irwin, Illinois.

Smail, R. (1986a), 'The Great Poverty Cover-Up', *Low Pay Review*, no. 27, pp. 24-27.

Smail, R. (1986b), 'The Pay Race - Winners and Losers', *Low Pay Review*, no. 28, pp. 4-10.

Stark, T. (1978), 'Personal Incomes', in W.F. Maunder (ed), *Reviews of United Kingdom Statistical Sources*, vol. VI, Pergamon Press, Oxford.

Stibbard, P.J. (1979), 'Consumer Credit', *Economic Trends*, no. 311, pp. 99-107.

Stone, J.R.N. (1954a), *The Measurement of Consumer Expenditure and Behaviour in the UK, 1920-38*, Cambridge University Press. Cambridge.

Stone, J.R.N. (1954b), 'Linear Expenditure Systems and Demand Analysis - an application to the pattern of British demand', *Economic Journal*, vol. 64, pp. 511-27.

Theil, H. (1965), 'The Information Approach to Demand Analysis', *Econometrica*, vol. 33, pp. 67-87.

Theil, H. (1980), *The System-Wide Approach to Microeconomics*, North-Holland, Amsterdam.

Toland, S. (1981), 'Committed and Discretionary Savings', *Economic Trends*, no. 337, pp. 109-35.

Townend, J.C. (1976) 'The Personal Savings Ratio', *Bank of England Quarterly Bulletin*, vol. 16, pp. 53-73.

Townsend, P. (1979), *Poverty in the United Kingdom*, Penguin, London.

Ungern-Sternberg, T. von (1981), 'Inflation and Savings: International Evidence on Inflation Induced Income Losses', *Economic Journal*, vol. 91, pp. 961-76.

Wall, K.D., A.J. Preston, J.W. Bray and M.H. Peston (1975), 'Estimates of a Simple Control Model of the U.K. Economy', in G.A. Renton (ed), *Modelling the Economy*, Heinemann, London.

White, M. (1983) *Long-term Unemployment and Labour Markets*, Policy Studies Institute, London.

Zellner, A (1962), 'An Efficient Method of Estimating Seemingly Unrelated Regressions and Tests for Aggregation Bias', *Journal of the American Statistical Association*, vol. 57, pp. 348-68.

Index